MASTERING
^{THE} **PREMIER LEAGUE**

MASTERING

THE PREMIER LEAGUE

THE TACTICAL CONCEPTS BEHIND
PEP GUARDIOLA'S MANCHESTER CITY

LEE SCOTT

First published by Pitch Publishing, 2019

Pitch Publishing
A2 Yeoman Gate
Yeoman Way
Worthing
Sussex
BN13 3QZ
www.pitchpublishing.co.uk
info@pitchpublishing.co.uk

A CIP catalogue record is available for this book
from the British Library.

ISBN 978-1-78531-563-3

Typesetting and origination by Pitch Publishing
Printed and bound in India by Replika Press Pvt. Ltd.

Contents

For Kelly, Alex, Thomas and Harry. Your love and support means everything.

Introduction

In retrospect, the genesis of this book was actually some time ago. I was writing on a semi-regular basis for a couple of well-known websites and my writing, predominantly based on the tactical side of the game, was well received. I was contacted by someone that I knew only through social media, a man named Chris Darwen, who had the idea of starting a new website that would focus on the tactical side of the game. Chris wanted to know if this was something that I would be interested in. Well, of course I was: the opportunity to write in the way that I wanted to about the subject that fascinated me was too good to turn down. This site would come with financial backing and as such Chris wanted me to write a manifesto for the site that would sell the idea to the investors.

This was the first time that I had ever had to sit down and consider why I actually write the way that I do. I was lucky enough to have been invited to join the fantastic tactical website *Spielverlagerung* but my writing there never took off. I realised that I did not fit with the philosophy of why they write. The incredibly talented group at *SV* write in order to educate themselves. The readers are important, to an extent, but the overriding 'why' for their site was to further their own self-improvement. I should be clear that I am in no way being critical of this idea and the talent that has written on that site is astounding. I am still an avid reader whenever a new post is released.

What then was my 'why'? I realised that I wanted to show people that the idea of tactical concepts and trends was not overly complicated. I wanted to simplify elements of the language that surrounds this side of the game and make it accessible to all of those that were interested but did not know where or how to start understanding. That was the core of the manifesto that I created and that process has now led to the magnificent *Total Football Analysis* website and to my being able to call Chris a friend.

I first fell in love with the football of Pep Guardiola, as so many others did, when the Spaniard was coaching FC Barcelona. Guardiola changed the world of football with that team and introduced to many the concept of controlling and manipulating space as his side progressed towards the opposition goal via a series of short passes that mesmerised the opposition and those watching alike.

Not only did Guardiola change the way that football was viewed from the inside; he also did the same for those of us watching from afar. The prism through which we viewed football was changed forever.

When Guardiola left Barcelona and eventually joined Bayern Munich we saw a new side of the Spanish coach. He assimilated into German football and took some aspects of the game there and introduced them into his game model.

If his time at Barcelona gave us Lionel Messi and the false nine, then Bayern Munich gave us Philipp Lahm and the inverted full-back. Guardiola seemed to be capable of finding new solutions to ensure that key spaces were always occupied and exploited and he did so in new and creative ways.

Then it was time for Guardiola to take his fascinating game model to these shores as coach of the already impressive Manchester City. After a difficult first season in charge, in which the coach learnt a lot about certain aspects of the British game, we then saw Manchester City blow apart the majority of their opposition over the course of the 2017/18 and 2018/19 seasons. The former saw the team set records for points gained and the latter saw them perform at such a high level that they retained their Premier League title despite Liverpool performing incredibly well and running them so close that the league was decided on the last day of the season.

Now feels like the right time to take all that I have learnt about Guardiola over the years and try to explain just what makes City so effective on the pitch.

There are those, of course, who will point at the levels of spending and suggest that without significant levels of financial backing Guardiola could not be successful. While the capacity of City to spend is largely unmatched in the football world it does not take into account the ability of Guardiola to improve players. Under his coaching we see good players become great and great players become world class. This is what Guardiola brings you, a level of detailed thinking on and off the pitch that can improve the performances of each player by the ten per cent needed to make his club successful.

We have often heard stories throughout his career from former players detailing the way that Guardiola would prepare them for games. The predictions that he would make to his

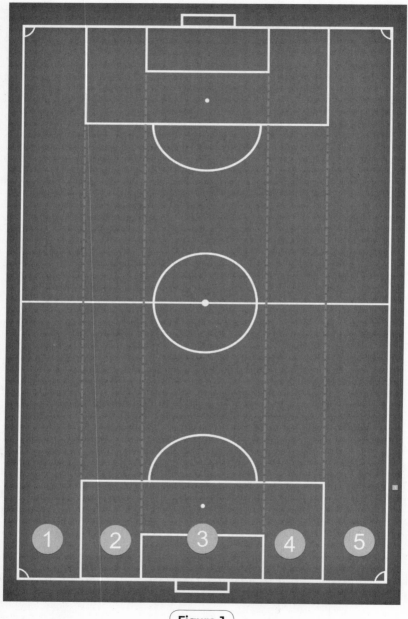

Figure 1

players before games of how the opposition would set up and how they would react to City, almost always came true.

The tactical concepts used most often by City are relatively simple when broken down. What makes them so effective, however, is the way that they execute these concepts with unerring efficiency. Over the course of this book, I hope to be able to offer you a clear insight into why and how City move and pass the way that they do. At the end of the book if you are now able to enjoy the style of play used by Guardiola even just a little more, then I will judge my efforts to have been a success.

Firstly, before we get into the tactical concepts promised, I want to introduce you to a small piece of language that you may already be familiar with through your own reading or writing. That is the often misunderstood 'half-space'. This term is one that I use throughout my writing and I have done so for some time now. There are some, especially on social media, who consider it to be useless jargon. In fact, it is an integral part of understanding the tactical concepts of Guardiola and Manchester City and it is not at all complicated.

In *figure 1* we see an image of a pitch that I have used to create all of the images for this book. The pitch is split into five vertical channels that are labelled from one to five from left to right. Channels two and four are the half-spaces. They refer to areas of the field that Pep Guardiola likes to have occupied when his team are in the attacking phase. If they do so properly then the opposition are forced to move from their defensive position to cover these areas and that opens space elsewhere. See, not complicated at all.

Chapter 1

Playing Out from the Back

It has become a common sight when watching Manchester City under Pep Guardiola to see the central defenders and goalkeeper engaging in periods of combination football that would not be out of place around the opposition penalty area. Such is the ability with the ball that these players possess, they are able to receive the ball in tight areas under extreme pressure.

We saw the importance placed on this concept by Guardiola in the way that he approached the goalkeeper position upon being appointed. The first choice goalkeeper at City when the Spaniard took charge was England international Joe Hart. It took no time at all for Guardiola to assert that Hart would not be part of his plans; there were huge doubts surrounding his ability to play with the ball at his feet under pressure.

Initially, we saw City turn to Barcelona, and they signed Chilean international Claudio Bravo. Unfortunately, this move proved to be largely disastrous and by the start of the 2017/18 season, the club were forced back into the transfer market again, this time securing the signature of the Brazilian international Ederson from Portuguese giants Benfica.

So far in his career in England, we have seen Ederson gain plaudits not only for his shot-stopping ability but also for his distribution and ability to contribute to the build-up phase.

The ability to control possession in the attacking phase from the defensive third is a key concept for the game model installed by Guardiola at City.

In order for them to be able to play forward through the thirds and create opportunities in the final third, the initial ball out from the back has to be clean. In order to achieve this clean ball progression, there are certain automatic movements that we see time and time again from City depending on the numerical match-ups faced by their defensive players. If the opposition only commits one player to press the ball in the initial moments then the build-up is fairly simple as the two central defenders split to the sides of the penalty area and form a wide triangle with the goalkeeper and outplay the pressing player. When the opposition starts to press with more players then the situation becomes progressively more complex. Two pressing players will see the deepest sitting midfielder drop back to give a passing option and provide numerical superiority for the pass. A third pressing player sees a further option added for City with either a full-back or one of the two more advanced central midfielders dropping back in order to secure the clean progression of the ball. Indeed, there is a simple formula to the idea behind this style of ball progression: the +1 rule.

In order to secure the ball and enable the play to develop from the defensive third into the more advanced areas, City need to create numerical superiority over their opponents.

The basic idea, therefore, is to have at least one more player offering passing options from the first moment of the build-up of play than the opposition has committed to pressing the ball. This should always ensure that there is at least one free player available to receive a pass.

There are, of course, exceptions to this rule: there are some opponents, Liverpool for example, who press intelligently using angled runs that allow one pressing player to cover two City players. When faced with sides that adopt a more intelligent pressing model we tend to see City use more complex rotations to ensure that they are still able to play through the press.

It is important to note that the above does not mean that City look to play the short pass out from the goalkeeper every single time. With Ederson in goal, there is the option to play a slightly more direct pass over a medium range that can bypass the press and find a player in space behind the opposition press. This option is contrary to the belief that many people held after Guardiola's first season at City that the Spaniard was so focused on a single model of play that he would not allow any deviation from that model. Instead, we see City adopt a flexible approach to their game model, in possession, that can be adapted depending on the tactical approach that is used by the opposition. This makes it far more difficult for opposing coaches to develop and install an effective defensive game plan when they are preparing to face City. Should they press high and in numbers and give up the medium pass over the top to the full-backs or central midfielders? Or should they drop slightly deeper and allow City to progress the ball from the goalkeeper in a clean and easy manner? Now, after three seasons in the Premier League, the majority of coaches, and even casual fans and pundits, can see what City want to do at the beginning of their attacking phase. The issue is that reacting to stop one aspect of the City build-up leaves you wide open to another. You are essentially damned if you do and damned if you don't.

It is this impossible choice that makes it so difficult to play against this City side and to prevent them from securing safe possession of the ball. There are times in which sides will adopt a high press against City as they are progressing the ball up from the first third. It is a mark of the importance that Guardiola places on this concept that the coach is willing to allow for his defensive players to make mistakes when playing out in this manner.

In the early stages of his tenure as coach, there were points in the season where the media were critical of the mistakes made by the central defender John Stones in particular. Whenever Guardiola was questioned by these media outlets about the mistakes being made by the young defender, the coach was vocal in his support for the players, stating that any mistakes were the responsibility of the coaching staff who were working in training to implement their game model. This support from Guardiola and the other first-team coaches allowed the players in the defensive unit to learn and assimilate all of the information being fed to them in a safe environment. It would have been easy for the players to have taken the criticism on board and then started playing more direct passes whenever they came under pressure. Instead, they remained calm and kept trying to play out through pressure until it became second nature for them.

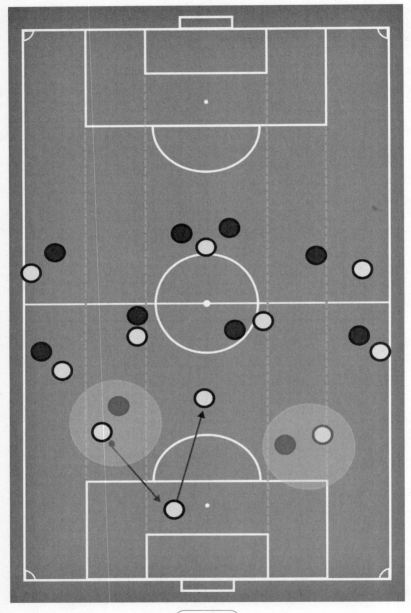

Figure 2

The most important aspect of this tactical concept is the ability for City to develop numerical superiority against their opponent when they are looking to build up from the back. This means, very simply, that they need to have one more player in a position to receive the ball than the opposition has applying pressure.

In *figure 2*, we see a simple example of City in possession of the ball just outside their penalty area. Both central defenders are closely marked but the man in possession, the left-sided central defender, is able to use the supporting position of Ederson in goal to play back. It is at this point that we see the first part of the concept really come into play. While the two central defenders are being engaged, the number '6' is not. The two defenders will split into wider positions, aware that this will drag the two opposition attackers with them, and this will leave Ederson with a simple vertical pass through to the '6' as he drops centrally.

The concept works the same way if City have a 3v2 situation but the pressure is on one central defender and the '6'. The free man will simply drop into a pocket of space so that they can receive the pass and play out of the press. If the opposition press with more than two players then one of the full-backs or one of the two central midfielders then comes into play in order to ensure that City continue to have the numerical advantage.

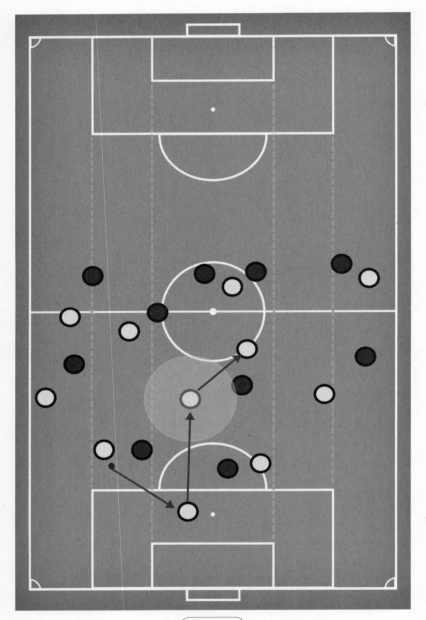

Figure 3

In *figure 3* we see a somewhat similar example with the '6' once again operating as the free man when City are trying to build out from their defence. The same principle applies as the ball is first passed back into Ederson before the Brazilian goalkeeper escapes the pressure with a vertical pass to the '6'. This time, however, the pass is riskier as the space between the two central defenders, and therefore the pressing opponents, is much tighter.

It is only logical to think that a large part of the recruitment plan that led City to sign Ederson prior to the 2017/18 season was the ability of the Brazilian to contribute with his feet. It is situations like this that informed this decision. As Ederson takes possession, the structure ahead of him is actually relatively set. The two full-backs have advanced forward, but only to the same line as the '6'. This 'line' refers to a horizontal line across the pitch. Most attacking structures involve players positioning themselves on lines that allow for the ball to be progressed using passes at different angles. Here, in order to secure the safe progression of the ball, the two full-backs are ready to drop back, either centrally or wide, in order to provide a passing option to bypass the press.

As the ball is progressed from Ederson to the '6' he is then able to simply turn away from pressure and feed the ball forward to a more advanced team-mate. All of this is possible due to the knowledge that the City players have of the angles and lines they need to occupy.

As the ball is progressed into higher areas of the field, the role that Ederson plays in enabling the progression of the ball is lessened. Instead, the '6' and the two full-backs take on a greater role. This is especially true when Kyle Walker plays at right-back and Aymeric Laporte at left-back. Both can be seen moving inside in order to receive the ball on the same line as the central defenders, to allow for the ball to be played forward.

On occasions, it can look as though City are passing the ball without real purpose when they rotate the ball across the defensive line. In fact, each player receiving the ball looks for a vertical pass into the midfield as a priority before moving the ball across once more. If the clear pass into the midfield, often beyond the line of pressure, is not on then the ball moves to the next man.

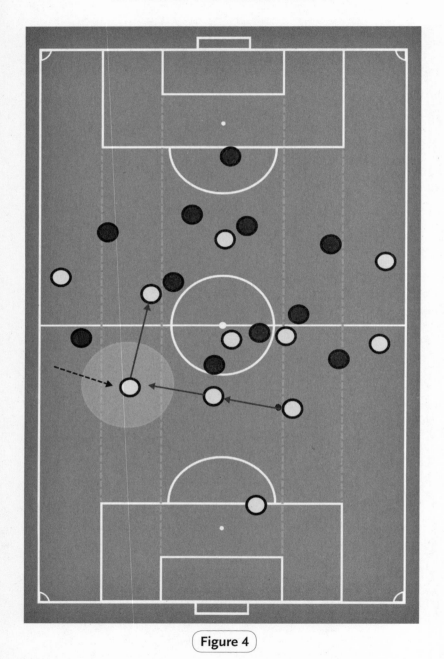

Figure 4

In *figure 4* we see the ball being shifted across to the left-back who has moved infield slightly to occupy the left half-space. This small piece of movement allows the left-back to receive the ball and then play forward to the central midfielder who is on a higher line in the same half-space. With the opposition defensive block concentrated on the opposite side of the field, City are able to bypass it due to the speed at which the ball is moved across and then forward.

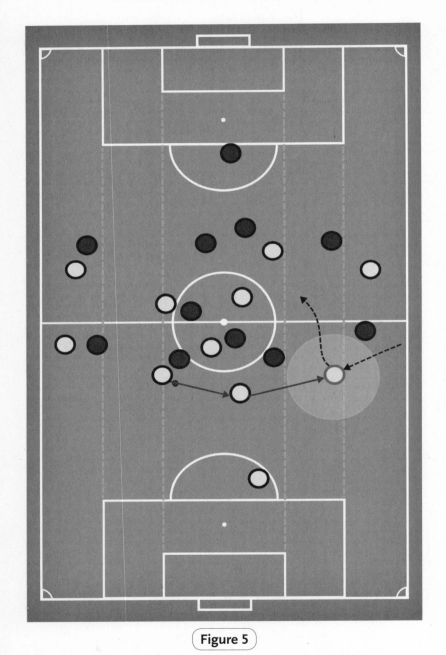

Figure 5

While at left-back Aymeric Laporte is a more cautious player who will look to distribute the ball in the first instance, Kyle Walker is more likely to use other options with which to progress the ball forwards. In *figure 5* we see the ball being cycled across the defensive line once again. As the ball reaches Walker, however, this time instead of passing forwards beyond the line of pressure, he would drive forward in possession of the ball and dribble past the defensive block of the opposition. Having a player capable of carrying the ball in this manner from the defensive line is hugely beneficial, as a single player running with the ball can force the opposition defenders to have to move out of position in order to engage the ball. This movement then creates space in behind that can be exploited by the more advanced players for City.

We often see City use this method of forcing the opposition defensive block to engage often when the other team are trying to sit in a deep and passive block, meaning they are unwilling to press and be caught out of position. City will use their full-backs or even their central defenders to dribble forward with the ball. As soon as the opposing defenders move out to engage the space that they have vacated, they will be ruthlessly exploited by the more creative players in the City squad.

A player such as Walker collecting possession on the same line as the defenders represents a dual threat for the opposition. He is capable of driving forward, as seen above, or passing through the lines into advanced areas. This tactical understanding of the game model implemented by Pep Guardiola explains why Walker has been a mainstay in this team under the City boss.

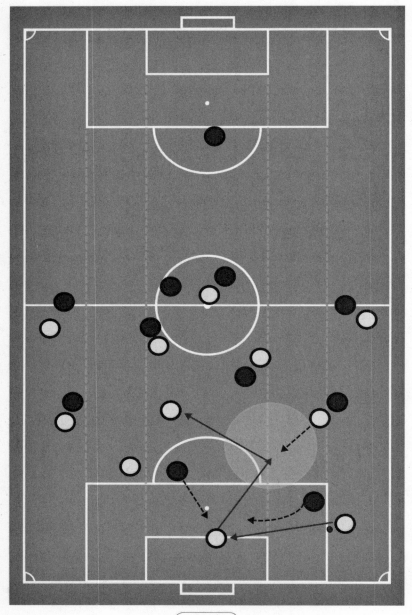

Figure 6

As we touched upon previously, there are times when looking to progress the ball that City use the full-backs to move the ball cleanly past the opposition block. In *figure 6* the ball is originally with the deepest defender. He is under pressure and so accesses the supporting position given by Ederson in goal. Normally in this situation with two opposition attackers pressing, we would see City create a numerical advantage using the '6'. The opposition attacker on the far side, however, is pressing the pass to the goalkeeper and he angles his run to cover both the second central defender and the '6'.

With more time the second central defender would drop quickly to the wide section of the penalty area. This would allow the goalkeeper to escape the press and retain possession. With the press from the forward coming too quickly, the goalkeeper has to react quicker. The right-back then drops back into the right half-space where he creates a clear passing lane that the goalkeeper can use to progress the ball.

We often see City make these movements with the ball first coming out to a player occupying the half-space before moving into the central areas, either to the '6' or to one of the two more advanced central midfielders.

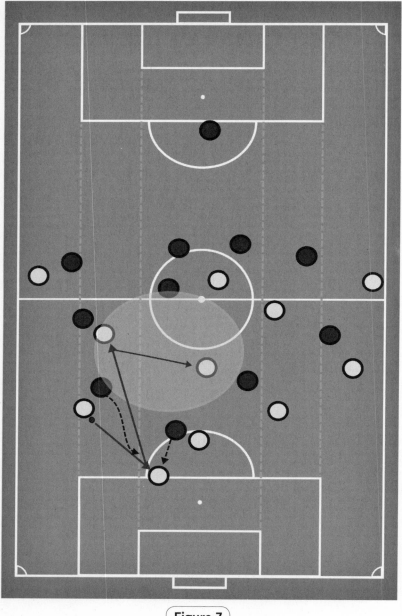

Figure 7

With the passing ability of Ederson in goal, the manner with which City progress the ball from the back is greatly altered. His ability to use the ball allows City to create structures that let them outplay the opposition from a variety of positions. In *figure 7* the opposition press is once again preventing City from easily playing out.

The angle and proximity of the two pressing players again means that Ederson has to play quickly to avoid being closed down and potentially losing the ball.

The movement in order to create the passing lane and allow the ball to be played through this time comes from the central midfielder, who drops back from his advanced position into the half-space to receive the pass through. The pass when it is made splits between the two pressing players for the opposition and once again City are able to play into more advanced areas comfortably, bypassing opposition players who have allowed themselves to be forced out of position.

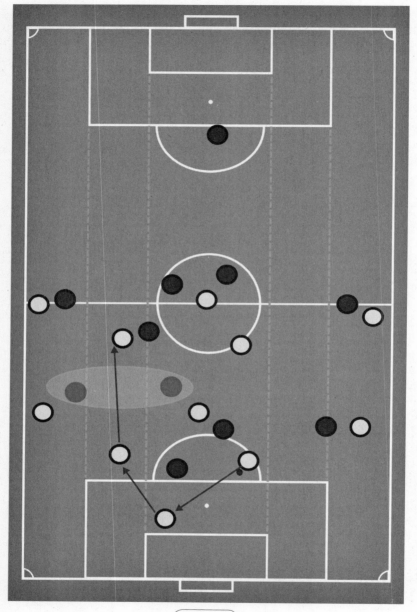

Figure 8

The final aspect of this concept that we need to discuss comes in the desire of City to progress the ball forwards into the central areas while breaking the lines of the opposition through vertical passes. In *figure 8* we clearly see this in action. Once again the initial pass comes back from a central defender to Ederson. As the goalkeeper takes possession of the ball he is able to open his body and play out to the second central defender around the pressing players.

It is at this point that City will look to play forward into more advanced areas of the field. The opposition defensive structure is not compact and they have allowed themselves to be pulled up to apply pressure to City. As the central defender takes possession of the ball he is able to turn upfield under little immediate pressure.

There are two opposition players ahead of the man in possession on the same line. The central defender is able to play a vertical pass between these two players that splits their line of pressure and finds the more advanced central midfielder in space behind them. As soon as this pass is completed, City have created an advanced platform from which they can launch their attacking move. These advanced platforms behind the opposition lines are incredibly effective for City.

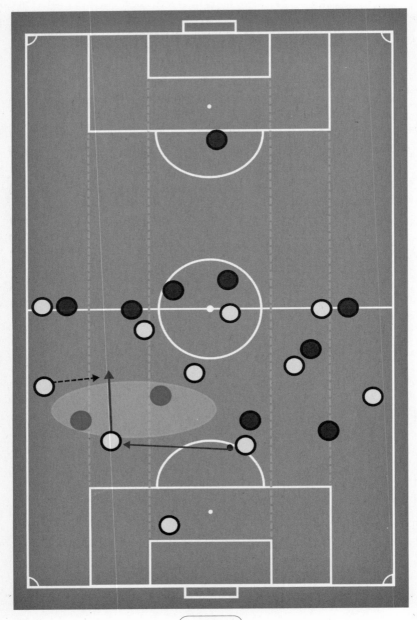

Figure 9

Figure 9 shows a similar situation with the ball this time progressed across between the two central defenders. This time as the left-sided central defender takes possession of the ball he is faced with two opposition players in close proximity to him. These players, however, are not compact and a clever piece of movement from the left-back allows the ball to be easily played through this line into space.

As the central defender takes possession of the ball, the left-back makes a small lateral movement from the wide area into the left half-space. This movement creates a passing lane for the man in possession through the two closest defensive players. As soon as the pass connects with the full-back they are able to collect the ball and either drive through towards the halfway line or continue with the passing move upfield.

These small tactical movements allow Manchester City to effectively and safely progress the ball forward and through the opposition. The most clever aspect of these pieces of play is that they are so flexible. Whatever the opposition choose to do in order to press the ball we see City having an answer. They create numerical advantages that allow them to play forward into central areas and use clever positioning in order to create passing lanes for the goalkeeper or central defenders to use.

The concepts used by City in these areas are not complicated, and nor should they be, but this does not mean that they are easily stopped. There are some teams who will press high and hard in an attempt to prevent City from playing out of these areas; this is when we see Ederson accessing his range of passing to play the ball over the press into central areas.

Chapter 2
Role of the Full-Backs

There are few positions within football that have experienced a more radical change over the course of the last decade than that of the full-backs. Traditionally, full-backs were seen as players who would perform largely defensive functions with the occasional incursion into the opposition half. Now, the modern full-back is expected to perform the same actions in the attacking phase that were typically reserved for wingers.

Full-backs offer width in the attacking third and offer options to combine with their attacking team-mates in order to progress the ball forward.

These changes are the result of the decreased space in central areas with players becoming fitter and stronger due to improvements in training and sports science. As space became tighter in the middle we gradually saw full-backs become the only players on the pitch who could receive the ball with space to advance forward. In order to accommodate this intrinsic change to the position, the technical attributes needed to play full-back changed to reflect the greater need to provide an attacking threat.

While full-backs would still receive the ball in space in the defensive and middle thirds, they would also need to be able to receive the ball in tight spaces in the final third. Indeed, there began a trend of wingers moving back to play as full-backs given their natural inclination to operate in high positions when their side were in the attacking phase. The belief ran that you could teach an attacking player to defend but it was more difficult to adequately teach a defensive player to operate as an attacking player.

The full-back positions have always been important within a Pep Guardiola side. When Guardiola was in charge of Barcelona we saw the Brazilian international Dani Alves become arguably the best full-back in the world, albeit while operating effectively as a right-winger in the possession-heavy system of the Spanish side. At Bayern Munich, we saw Guardiola adapt his use of the position with Philipp Lahm and David Alaba.

While full-backs had previously been largely linear in that they had primarily operated in wide areas, this was the first time that we saw full-backs utilised in an inverted position. When in possession of the ball – which was the majority of the time! – the width was provided by the wingers staying in high areas on the outside. The full-backs would then move into central areas in order to provide secure possession of the ball. The ball-near (on the same side as the ball) full-back would retain a traditional position, although more narrow than normal, while the ball-far full-back would move into the centre of the midfield.

This ensured that Bayern always had control of the central areas of the pitch and the player in possession had players in support to offer passing options. This positional switch was also designed to create the opportunity for the likes of Thiago to push forward from his midfield position to operate between the lines of the opposition midfield and defence.

When Guardiola agreed to take over as coach of Manchester City in 2016 there was widespread excitement to see the inverted full-back in English football. What we saw instead, however, was that Guardiola was a more nuanced and flexible coach than we had been led to believe.

There were occasions in his first season when the full-backs, namely Pablo Zabaleta, Gael Clichy, Bacary Sagna, Aleksandar Kolarov and Jesus Navas, played in their traditional wide positions. In other matches, depending on the opposition, those full-backs were used in inverted roles. There was one significant issue as a result of these full-back options: a lack of genuine quality. All five players used in these positions most often in that season by City were in the later stages of their career. New blood was needed and this resulted in a significant transfer outlay prior to the 2017/18 season with Benjamin Mendy, Kyle Walker and Danilo all signed to refresh the full-back area of the squad.

The result was instantaneous, with City looking like a Guardiola team almost from the very start of the Spaniard's second season in charge. While his first year was spent acclimatising to an unfamiliar football culture, the second and third years were spent shaping that culture in Guardiola's own image. A large part of this was down to the performances of these new full-backs, who were the final pieces in the tactical puzzle that unlocked the attacking potential of this City side.

At Barcelona, the full-backs under Guardiola were used in a traditional role and at Bayern Munich they were used in inverted positions. Now, at Manchester City, this has evolved to the point that the full-backs perform hybrid roles. Switching from the wide positions to positions in the half-spaces or central zones, sometimes in the same match. We see matches in which one full-back is used to support the attack in wide areas while the other retains a deep line to almost form a back three. This flexibility demands that the players who play in the full-back positions retain a great deal of tactical information. This is a constant process of improvement from Guardiola and his coaching team, with the players in question having to understand when and how to move in and out of certain zones in order to meet the demands of the game model.

As such, the type of full-back who thrives in a system under Guardiola is very specific. The likes of Walker and Mendy can be viewed as fairly typical full-backs. With Fabian Delph and Oleksandr Zinchenko also playing at left-back, however. the skillset provided by these two players, predominantly midfielders, gives a different interpretation of the role. Indeed, through the entire game model of Guardiola, you can easily make the argument that the full-back positions are amongst the most complicated to learn and play well. This goes some way to explaining why the Spaniard struggled in his early period in charge at City where the full-backs were ageing and unable to perform the role as their coach required.

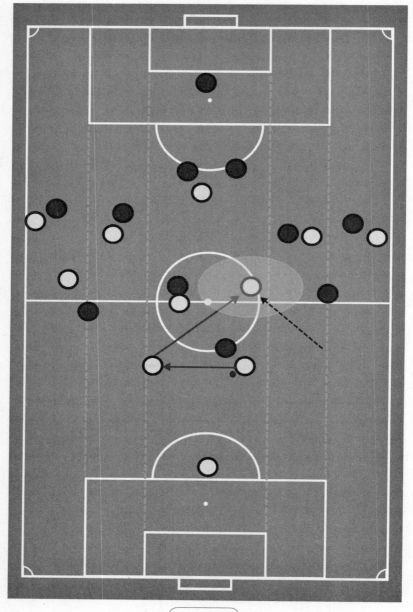

Figure 10

A key part of the game model used by Guardiola throughout his coaching career, whether at Barcelona, Bayern Munich or now at Manchester City, has been the ability to control and dominate the central areas of the pitch. The problem that Guardiola had when he moved away from Barcelona is that he did not have another Xavi, a player with the capacity to control space across the central areas with constant passing and movement. Instead, he had midfielders who were more comfortable occupying spaces in the final third, such as David Silva or Kevin De Bruyne. This meant that he had to create more ways in which his players could occupy central spaces.

Hence the decision to have full-backs make diagonal runs into the central areas in order to create overloads and numerical superiority in these areas. In *figure 10* we see an example of these diagonal movements that are used by the full-backs at City. These are designed to occupy spaces but also to further aid ball progression up towards the final third.

With the left-sided central defender in possession of the ball the right-back — Kyle Walker, in this instance — made the diagonal run in order to create a passing lane that allowed City to progress the ball into the central areas. From these positions, the full-backs then provide a wide base from which City can create their attacking positions. With one or both of the full-backs moving centrally onto the same line as the '6' there are always supporting lines for City to play back into, if space in the final third is too compact. These positions from the full-backs also make it more difficult for the opposition to launch effective counter-attacks.

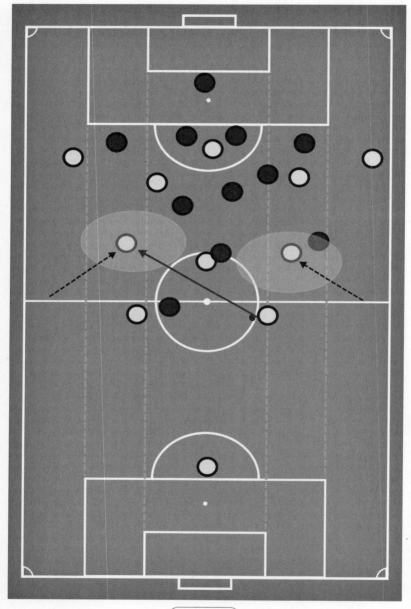

Figure 11

The movements in *figure 11* show the patterns that City use when they have both full-backs move into inverted positions to flank the '6'. The most important aspect of these movements is that they allow for the ball to be progressed forwards. This is always the first priority for a City player in possession in the defensive and central thirds of the pitch. Can they create opportunities to bypass lines of opposition pressure in order to cleanly progress the ball forwards? In the final third this priority shifts to be *Can I find the space to shoot?* or *Can I create the chance for someone else to shoot?* and indeed everything that we know about City from a tactical viewpoint should be viewed with this in mind. As the two full-backs moved inside to occupy the same line as the '6' in this example, the ball was played diagonally to the left-back, Fabian Delph, who had moved from the wide area into the left half-space.

Now City have the ball in space in the left half-space and the opposition defensive block will have to rotate over to cover the space. What is interesting is the shape that this piece of movement creates. City have a base of three players across that line but they have five forward players in advanced areas. These five players are able to spread out across the vertical lines, wide areas, half-spaces and central area. Now as the opposition block has to shift across, they will inevitably create spaces that can be used by these advanced players to create superiority in the final third.

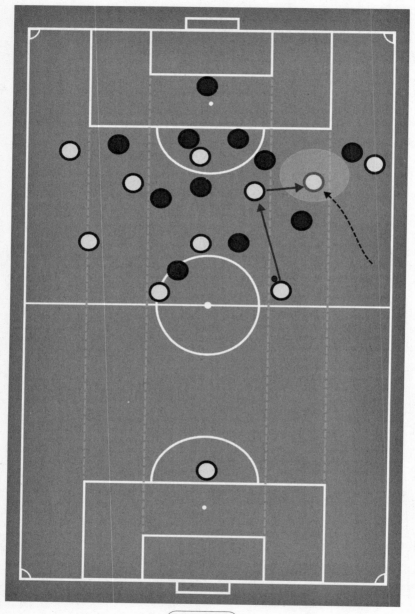

Figure 12

Another key aspect of the role of the full-back in the City system comes in their ability to move from defensive zones to fill spaces in the overall attacking structures. Depending on the players selected by Pep Guardiola to play in the wide attacker positions, the spaces that are open to being used by the full-backs are different. If the likes of Raheem Sterling or Leroy Sane play then they tend to hold a wide position, right on the line, in the initial movements of the attacking phase. This means that the spaces that are open are inside in the half-spaces. If someone like Bernardo Silva plays then he likes to occupy these half-spaces and the open areas for the full-back are wide.

These slight changes depending on personnel are just another layer of information that the full-backs have to process. In *figure 12* we see the ball being progressed initially from the defender to one of the advanced midfielders in a central position. The wide forward is holding the width and this stretches the defensive block of the opposition. By forcing a defensive player wide to cover the threat of the wide player, City effectively create a pocket of space in the half-space that can be filled. The right-back, Kyle Walker, makes another diagonal run, this time into a more advanced position, and he is able to take possession in a dangerous pocket of space in between the lines of the opposition.

These movements, from deeper positions into the pockets of space that have been created by the positioning of the more advanced players in the attacking system, can be key, especially when it comes to breaking down teams that look to sit in deep and compact defensive blocks.

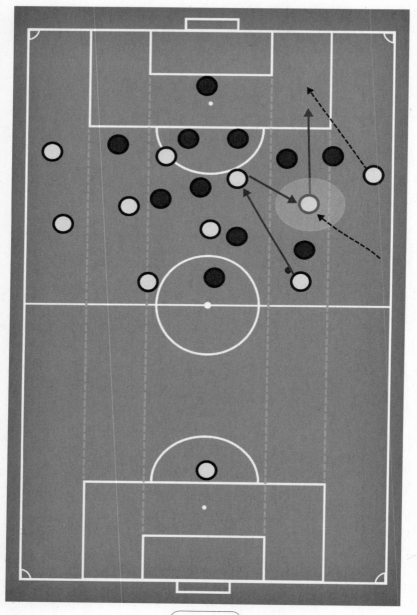

Figure 13

When the full-backs move into these areas in the half-spaces they are then able to connect with other attacking players to force overloads and create angles through which City can bypass the opposition defensive line.

In *figure 13* we again see Kyle Walker, from right-back, moving into the right side half-space in an advanced area. This time, as the ball is shifted forward to the central midfielder and then across to Walker in the half-space we see the difficulty that this position poses to the opposition. The initial forward pass to the central midfielder is timed with the movement of Walker diagonally. The fact that this pass and run occur at the same time makes it impossible for the closest defensive player to cover both threats. That defensive player is then effectively pinned in place when the ball is shifted across to Walker.

In these areas, the full-backs are released from strict scripted movements and they are free to create. In this instance, the ball is played between the defensive line into the penalty area and Raheem Sterling is able to make a diagonal run of his own in order to collect the ball.

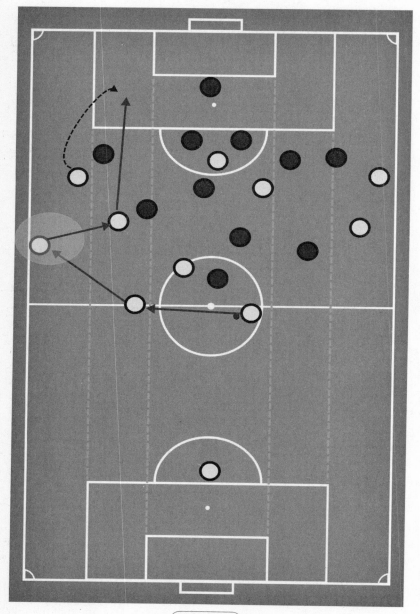

Figure 14

We are more likely to see Kyle Walker making these diagonal runs into advanced positions from right-back. On the left side, the typical positioning of the full-back is slightly deeper. This is in keeping with the differences of the two respective central midfielders. David Silva, typically on the left, likes to occupy the left half-space from where he can connect to the left wing. The role of the left-back then, when not inverted, is slightly different.

In *figure 14*, for example, we see the left-back holding the wide position, on the same line as the '6'. As the ball is shifted across the defensive line and out to the left-back, Fabian Delph in this instance, he is in a position to receive the ball in space. His options are either to play outside the wide player or to connect with the central midfielder. The aim is to release the wide player into the corner of the penalty area and as such the ball is played to David Silva. The Spaniard is then able to play the through ball to release the wide player.

From these positions, the left-back is therefore used in a more supporting role than the right-back would be. This is partially why the likes of Delph and Aymeric Laporte were so effective when played in the left-back role. The injury problems of Benjamin Mendy robbed Guardiola, for much of the 2018/19 season, of the attacking threat from left-back. Therefore the structure of the rest of the team had to adapt. Luckily this deeper role for the left-back suited the likes of David Silva perfectly with his preference to move out towards the wide areas.

The full-back position is, of course, important in football in general. The players in these positions will generally have time and space when they receive the ball with the ability to play forward without immediate pressure. Guardiola has taken the role of the full-backs to another level with the ability of the players in these areas to attack diagonally into either deep areas or into the advanced half-spaces.

These modern full-backs are a far cry from the purely defensive players that used to occupy these positions. Now they provide key attacking and defensive support which allows the full City team to operate as one unit. In order for the City full-backs to be able to adapt to the specific needs of each match, they need to have a wide and varied skillset but they also need to have a full understanding of the full game model that Guardiola uses. In many ways, you could argue that the full-back position is the most important for Manchester City.

Chapter 3

The Fernandinho Role

Any player who plays as the '6', at the base of the midfield three, for a Pep Guardiola side, must experience a sense of pressure. This was, after all, the role that Guardiola himself filled for the entirety of his career as he redefined the expectations of a player in that position. Traditionally, any player who filled this role was seen as a purely defensive player, responsible for breaking up attacks from the opposition and circulating the ball to more advanced players. As with so many things in football, however, this changed with Johan Cruyff and his insistence that the '6' become a key part in the attacking phase as well as the defensive.

As a player, Guardiola was asked at one point whether he preferred to play as a single pivot, as the lone player at the base of the midfield, or as a double pivot, with a second midfielder alongside him at the base. His answer was absolute: the single pivot. Guardiola believed unequivocally that a second player on the same line that he occupied would constrict the space available to him in possession of the ball and cut out vital passing lanes. This belief in the value of the single controlling midfielder at the base of the midfield is something that Guardiola carried through his playing career and into his coaching career.

When taking his formative steps as a coach with the Barcelona B side there was a sense that Guardiola perhaps got lucky in that he inherited a young talented '6' by the name of Sergio Busquets – although, it is perhaps only through the lens of hindsight that we can consider Guardiola to have been fortunate in this respect. There can be no question that Busquets has developed over the course of his career into a world class midfielder but at the same time, the impact that Guardiola had as a coach on the development of the player cannot be discounted.

At Barcelona B and then at Barcelona, Guardiola had a natural '6' at his disposal but it was at Bayern Munich that we saw Guardiola initially struggle to identify the player best suited to this integral role. At first, his fellow Spaniard Javi Martinez was tried but Guardiola quickly identified that his best role was as a central defender. Eventually, Guardiola settled on a combination of sorts with the likes of Xabi Alonso and Philipp Lahm each spending time in rotation as the '6'.

Busquets, Alonso, Lahm; three players who are amongst the very best of their generation. That a coach with the tactical acumen of Guardiola would choose players of their ability and importance to fill this role within his tactical system says much for the importance that he places on the '6'. Effectively, this player becomes the embodiment of the coach's game model on the field. So often under Guardiola, this player is the one who dictates the tempo and sets the pattern of attack in possession. While the creative players in more advanced areas perhaps get more attention for their decisive contributions, the role of the '6' under Guardiola simply cannot be overlooked.

At Manchester City, there has been little doubt about this position in the 4-3-3, with the Brazilian international Fernandinho firmly embedded in this position. Indeed, such has been the impact made by the former Shakhtar Donetsk midfielder he became arguably the player that City could least afford to lose. This was particularly apparent in the 2018/19 season where periods of injury and suspension left City unable to select Fernandinho. This is not to say that City does not have a squad capable of covering for this absence. In Ilkay Gundogan, for example, they have a player with extensive experience both at club and international level. When the German international fills in at the base of the midfield, though, there is still a noticeable drop off in effectiveness when compared to Fernandinho.

In order to understand the reasons behind this we first have to identify what it is exactly that the '6' is expected to do under Guardiola in this tactical system. For us to fully examine this we have to separate his regular football actions into two sections, the defensive phase and the attacking phase. The defensive phase relates to those periods of the game in which the opposition are in possession of the ball. While we have already stated previously that under Guardiola the '6' is not a player with purely defensive functions, this is still an essential part of the role. Often the player that sits in this role at the base of the midfield is responsible for closing space between the defensive line and the line created by the two central midfielders and wide forwards when they drop back to create a four. The single controlling midfielder will shift across the width of the penalty area to prevent the opposition from creating pockets of space in which their attacking players will move.

The '6' is also key when it comes to preventing the opposition from launching quick counter-attacks at the moment of transition for City from attack to defence. Indeed, in the 2018/19 season in particular, Fernandinho became infamous for his mastery of the dark arts of football. Often we would see the opposition transition stopped when Fernandinho committed small fouls to prevent the other team from moving the ball forward quickly. There is no doubt that these small fouls, sometimes referred to as 'professional fouls', were part of a set strategy for City. They were never as effective, however, when Fernandinho was not in the starting line-up.

In the attacking phase the '6' is responsible for providing the base for the attacking structure. When the full-backs either retain their traditional wide position or move forward to join the attack then the deepest midfielder is the only player at this base. He will constantly be positioned in such a way as to provide support to the players in advanced positions, and these positions also allow him to choose the opportune moments when he can join in with the attacking structure in the final third. This happens most often against teams that look to sit in a low and passive defensive block. Having the '6' move from a deeper position to join the attack with a later run can create an overload in central areas that will allow City to play through a stubborn defensive block.

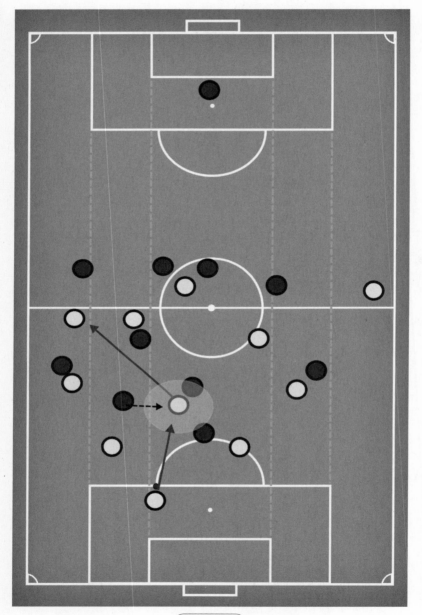

Figure 15

We have already seen the importance of the '6' when progressing the ball out from the defensive areas. He will drop in to provide numerical superiority in order to allow the ball to be progressed cleanly. In order to provide this function for the team, however, the player that fills this role has to be extremely press resistant. The term 'press resistance' simply refers to a player's ability to stay on the ball and manipulate it in tight areas when the opposition players are looking to apply pressure.

Press resistance is a key trait throughout this City side, where a willingness and ability to receive and play in tight areas is incredibly important when you look to progress the ball through the thirds . As you can see in *figure 15,* as Fernandinho takes possession of the ball there are three opposition players in close proximity and they look to press the ball. However, he has the quality and the composure to accept this pressure and then identify and use the passing lane to play out to the wide spaces.

The role of the '6' under Guardiola is of course to play as the pivot through which the play can be focused. This means that the player that fills this role has to have the vision and technical capacity to take the ball and then see the passing options ahead of him, as well as, of course, the technique to execute this pass. If you look again at *figure 15,* Fernandinho is able to play the ball out to Leroy Sane in the wide left position as opposed to trying to force the ball forward or even play a safer lateral pass out to the right side. When it comes to playing these slightly riskier passes forwards, it is clear that Guardiola and his coaching staff trust the players to make the right choice.

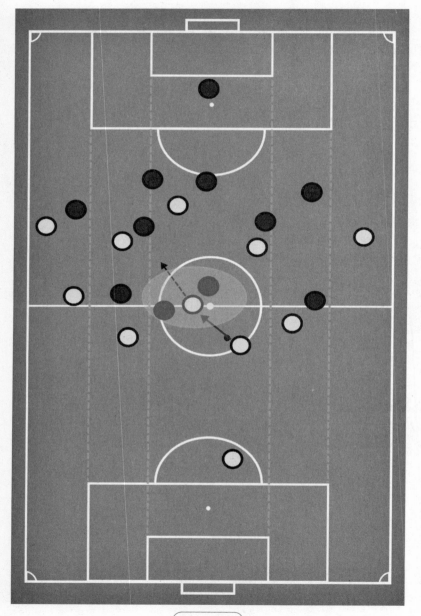

Figure 16

As discussed previously, there is more than one way for a player to break the line of the opposition with the ball. The most common way is for the ball to be passed between opposition players into players occupying space behind them. The other mechanism to accomplish this is for the player in possession of the ball to dribble through the line of pressure with the ball at their feet.

This is something that we see from Fernandinho when he takes possession of the ball with opposition pressure to the sides. The Brazilian is adept at disguising his turns on the ball to make the opposition think that he is going to take the first touch back towards his own goal. This touch, backwards, would provide a natural pressing trigger for many sides and opposition players would naturally be looking for this touch to act as a non-verbal signal to press forward.

Instead, as we can see in *figure 16,* Fernandinho received the ball from the central defender before shaping to take a touch but allowing the ball to run past him. In one movement he is able to move into the space behind the pressing opposition players.

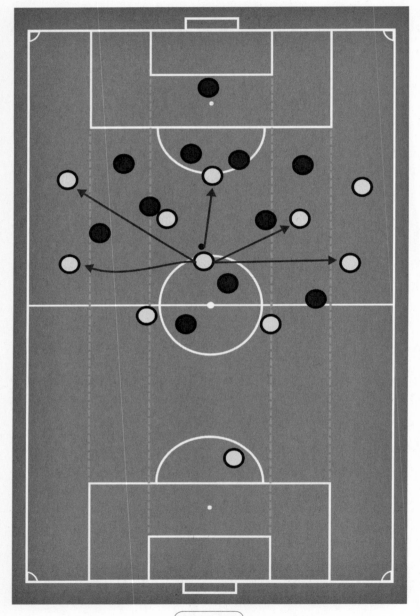

Figure 17

In *figure 17* we can see the importance of the '6' within the 4-3-3 structure as the central conduit that connects players across the entire tactical structure.

In the attacking phase we most often see this player positioned in the central lane where he is able to receive the ball either from deep areas or even back from more advanced areas before playing into team-mates who are in pockets of space. We have already seen, when discussing the progression of the ball from the back, that the priority for City in these areas is to find the clean passing lane in order to progress the ball forward to the next stage of the attack. The same concepts and priorities can be applied with the ball forward in more advanced areas. Indeed, we often see City enjoying large spells of possession with lengthy passing sequences with the ball in these areas. This is where the '6' acts as the central conduit for the side as a whole.

When Fernandinho occupies this position, his ability on the ball is often underrated. In fact he is an intelligent and capable passer of the ball who understands when to move the ball forward into the final third and when to play safer passes to retain possession. Often when Manchester City are in the middle of one of these passing sequences, it can seem as though they are passing the ball from side to side with no clear aim, passing the ball just for the sake of passing it. In fact, they are probing the defensive structure of the opponent and looking for opportunities to open up that will allow them to play the ball forward. The '6' is key in this as a player who usually has the whole of the attacking structure, and opposition defensive block, ahead of him. This allows the player in this position to clearly assess the positions of the opposition defensive players before deciding on how best to dictate the play when taking possession.

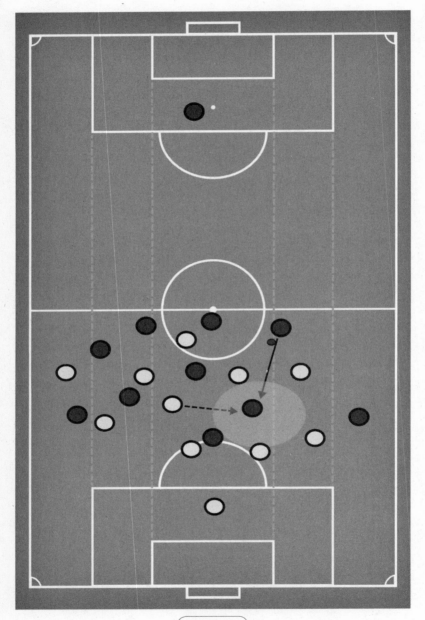

Figure 18

While we have already shown that the '6' under Guardiola has an important role to play in the attacking phase of the game, it is also important that we discuss the defensive responsibilities that this player has. At the beginning of this chapter we discussed in some detail the importance of the '6' in denying space to the opposition in the defensive third as the other team are attacking. This is shown in *figure 18*.

With the opposition attacking, the City structure has become something like a 4-1-4-1. It is important to note at this point that formations actually have very little bearing within the game model used by Guardiola. The overall shape at the start of the game is always 4-3-3 but beyond that the positions of the players will change in relation to the position of the ball on the pitch and the opposition.

As we see the opposition looking to attack, they have possession of the ball inside the City half on the right-hand side. As they look to play the ball forward we can see an opposition player has drifted into a pocket of space in between the line of the defence and the midfield for City. It is down to the '6' to be able to identify these threats and shift across to close down the space. This means that the space does not have to be directly defended by a midfielder, dropping deep, or by a defender who would have to step out. This allows City to keep their defensive shape and means that there are less obvious spaces in the lines that the opposition can exploit.

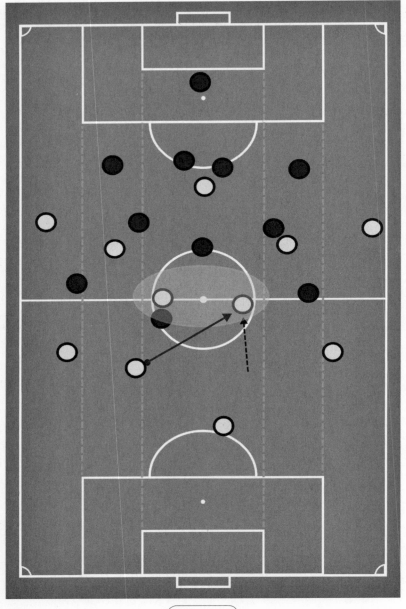

Figure 19

It is important to note that there were times, especially during the 2018/19 season, that City did actually effectively play with a double pivot. Not in the traditional sense of the position though: this came with a slight positional switch when City were in possession and during a period of games in which Fernandinho actually played as the right-sided central defender, with Ilkay Gundogan playing as the '6'.

When City were in possession of the ball we would see Gundogan shift across to the left side of the centre of the midfield. This would open up space for Fernandinho to step out of the defensive line to take up a position on the right side of the centre – you can see these movements in *figure 19*.

These movements were designed to allow Fernandinho to create additional passing lanes to enable the ball to be progressed out of the defensive line cleanly. This movement was used exclusively, however, against teams who did not press aggressively, and as such City were able to push Fernandinho into midfield to support Gundogan and leave a single central defender on the first line. This lack of immediate defensive support was mitigated somewhat by the ability of Ederson to take up a high position outside his penalty area to guard against the threat of quick opposition counter-attacks.

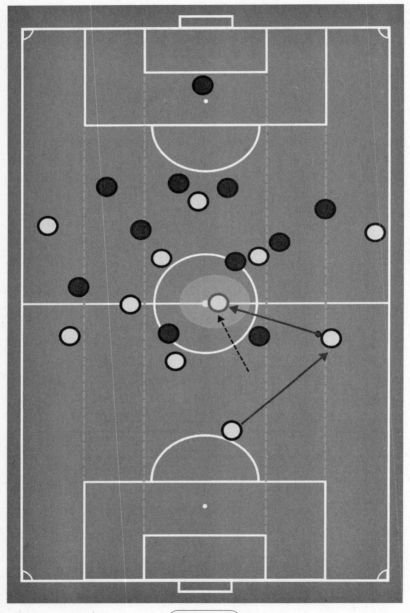

Figure 20

As we can also see in *figure 20,* this movement from Fernandinho forward to support Gundogan at the base of the midfield could be timed to provide periods of domination for City in the central areas.

As the ball was in the possession of the right-back, Kyle Walker, Fernandinho was able to step forward through the line of the opposition to create a passing lane for the full-back to find him with a diagonal pass. This pass, coupled with the movement of Gundogan away from the ball, produced an opportunity for City to create a central overload. By creating overloads in this manner, City would either be able to play through the opposition defensive block centrally or force the opposition to engage the ball by moving their defensive players out of position. As we have already discussed, any defensive player moving out of his position in the defensive block to engage the ball would create space elsewhere in the defensive block that could be exploited by City.

The willingness of Guardiola to develop this kind of movement into a double pivot flies in the face of those who say that the Spanish coach is too regimented in his tactical approach. He shows tactical flexibility and imagination that allow his side to dominate in possession of the ball in a manner that few clubs have managed in world football. The importance of the '6' in the overall structure is huge and it is expected that the club will look to recruit an understudy for Fernandinho in the near future in order to mitigate the threat of further injuries to the Brazilian.

Chapter 4

Overload and Isolate

Manchester City have, under Pep Guardiola, a well-deserved reputation as one of the most potent attacking sides in recent memory. In the 2017/18 season, City not only won 100 points, a Premier League record, but also scored 106 goals. In the 2018/19 season, those figures were 98 points and 95 goals.

At times, when they are in full flow, City have been irrepressible over the last two seasons, an attacking force with the capacity to score at almost any point when in possession of the ball.

Guardiola is known as a coach who demands very specific actions from his teams in the defensive phase. The manner in which City press and defend is drilled and defined by the coaching staff but in the attacking third the City players are allowed more freedom with which to express themselves. That is with one notable exception; regardless of the positioning of the ball at least one player is expected to retain a position wide on the opposite side of the field to the ball. This is an integral part of the most important attacking concepts used by this City side: overloading and isolation.

Fernandinho breaks through the Crystal Palace defence

John Stones covers the dangerous Eden Hazard at Stamford Bridge

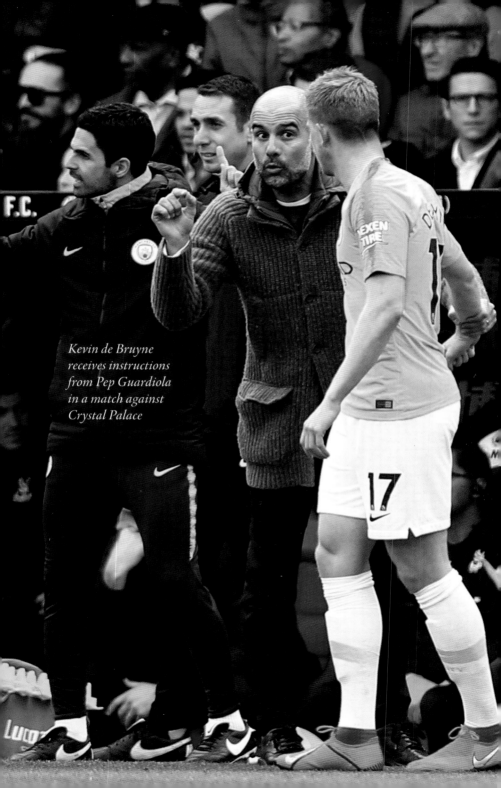

Kevin de Bruyne receives instructions from Pep Guardiola in a match against Crystal Palace

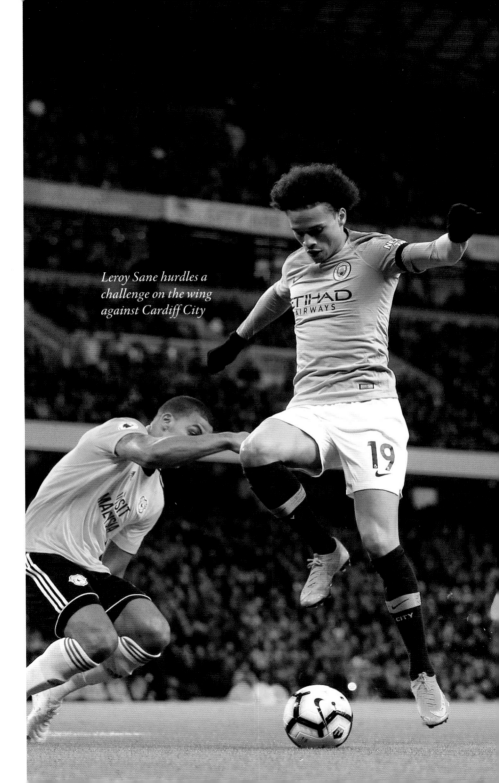

Leroy Sane hurdles a challenge on the wing against Cardiff City

Manchester City players rush to celebrate with goalscorer Sergio Aguero

Kyle Walker battles with two Everton players at Goodison Park

Leroy Sane is poised to strike whilst coming under pressure against Burnley

Raheem Sterling driving forward in possession against Leicester City

David Silva involved in the midfield battle against Manchester United

City players crowd around forward Raheem Sterling to celebrate his goal versus Watford

Coach Pep Guardiola celebrates victory for Manchester City versus Burnley

French defender Aymeric Laporte rises highest to head for goal against Brighton and Hove Albion

The concept of overloading is a relatively simple one as City look to, while in possession of the ball to create situations in which they have a numerical advantage over their opponents in a set area of the field. When viewed through the lens of positional play this meets one of the criteria set out in our introduction as City look to create a numerical superiority over their opponents.

The primary method preferred by Guardiola for doing so is relatively simple as City look to move the ball quickly and often over short areas in order to create passing networks and bypass the lines of opposition pressure. One regular pattern from City sees them create overloads on the left-hand side of the field with the left-sided central midfielder, usually David Silva, shifting into the left half-space and forming a triangle with the left-winger and the left-back. These three players are then supported by the holding midfielder and the left-sided central defender to create a strong attacking structure down that side. This structure allows City to quickly and safely switch the ball through players in order to play through the lines and create attacking opportunities. If, however, City cannot play through the opposition using the overload, usually because of a particularly active defensive opponent, they access the second concept explained in this chapter, isolation.

A common accusation levelled at a Guardiola side is that they seem to pass the ball just for the sake of passing it. Often we see two players making a series of short and quick passes between themselves and it seems as though there is no thought behind these passes other than shifting the ball slightly. These passes are in fact designed to draw the opposition over towards the ball. Each pass draws the opposition slightly over towards the ball and further constricts the space on the ball side of the field. The idea behind this concept is to create an opportunity on the ball far-side of the field where the side can have an attacking player isolated in a 1v1 opportunity against an opponent. As the opposition are pulled across closer to the ball, fearing the overload, the ball can then be played diagonally across to the opposite side. When isolated 1v1 against a direct defensive opponent, the likes of Raheem Sterling, Leroy Sane, Bernardo Silva and Riyad Mahrez are extremely difficult to contain. This is why under Guardiola the clear instruction in the attacking phase is to keep at least one wide player out on the ball far-side of the field, right against the touchline. Without that instruction, the switch of play from the overloading section of the field into the isolated side would be far less effective.

This concept was used to an extent by Guardiola while at Barcelona, with the likes of Thierry Henry positioned hard against the left-hand side of the field to stretch the defensive structure of the opposition. Guardiola perfected this practice at Bayern Munich where, along with the idea of inverted full-backs, the overload and isolate concepts formed a key part of the attacking game model used at the German club. With the likes of Arjen Robben and Franck Ribery operating on the wings, it is perhaps no surprise that Bayern would use an attacking concept that favoured attacking in the wide areas.

The truth is that on their own the concepts of overload or isolation are far less effective than if you combine the two and utilise them together. A part of what makes Manchester City so difficult to defend against is that you cannot be sure which concept they use in any given attack in order to force a breakthrough. They may play through the overload using a series of quick passes in combination or they may draw you across before accessing the isolated player on the opposite side of the field.

These different concepts are successful because of the way that City train under Guardiola. In order to operate effectively in an overload situation, you have to be able to occupy space effectively. City position themselves staggered on different lines as they look to overload a section of the field. This effectively creates a series of triangles which connect the attacking players to one another and so in possession the man with the ball always has more than one option to pass to. As a result, the opposition are always struggling to effectively defend against them as the options appear to keep coming as the ball is progressed towards the penalty area. The opposition may think that they have denied City the space to play through on the overload, then all of a sudden the ball will be switched across to the opposite side of the field and the pace and angle of the City attack will shift instantly.

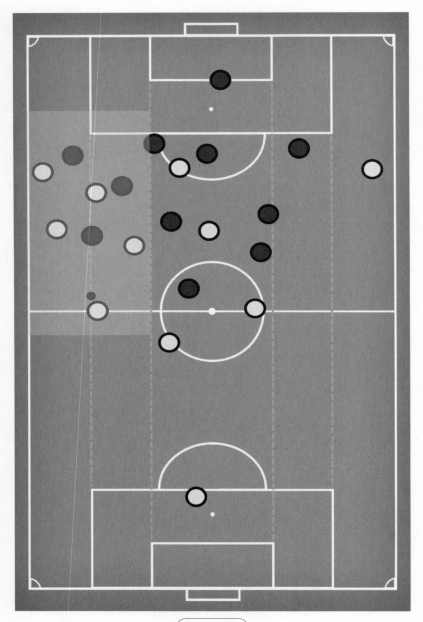

Figure 21

The idea behind creating the overloads required to comfortably play through the opposition is a reasonably simple one, and one that we have seen in a previous chapter when we looked at the way that City progress the ball from the defence. City will look to create numerical superiority over one or two of their vertical zones, with players positioned on slightly different lines in order to aid the progression of the ball forwards.

We can see this in *figure 21* as City have created a 5v3 situation over on the left side of the pitch. With Aymeric Laporte in possession of the ball as the left-sided central defender we see Fernandinho as the '6', and David Silva as the advanced '8', pressing across to the left side in order to give passing options. They have joined Oleksandr Zinchenko, at left-back, and Leroy Sane, at left wing.

It is worth noting that the forward player and second '8' have also pulled across slightly. They retain their positions in the central zone in order to allow the ball to be shifted centrally should the opportunity present itself. The structure is completed by Kyle Walker staying deep at right-back to offer balance and Bernardo Silva staying wide on the right-hand side.

Now the opposing team has a problem. If they try to collapse and remain compact then they run the risk of City being able to pass through them easily down the left-hand side. If they press then City will switch the ball centrally or over to the right-hand side. What we tend to see is that teams get caught between the two options and end up being drawn across to the overload without a strong defensive organisation. This allows City to essentially choose which way they will break through to goal.

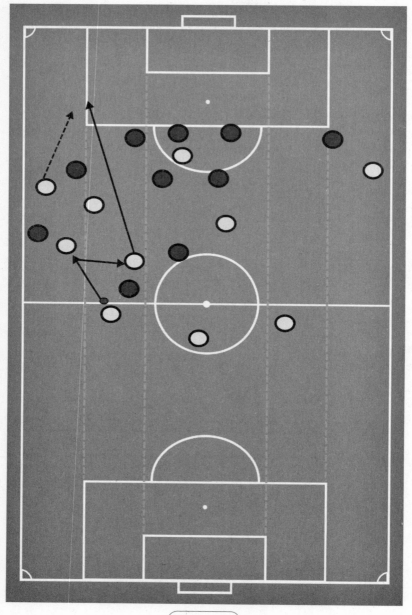

Figure 22

Guardiola is known to display incredible attention to detail during training sessions, which includes the positioning of players whether in or out of possession. He is known to demand absolute positional perfection, with his players expected to move in and out of zones depending on the position of the ball and the positioning of the rest of the team.

All of this work on the training pitch is designed to allow City to cut through opposition defensive structures like a knife will cut through butter. This is shown in *figure 22* as the ball moves from Aymeric Laporte, in possession originally, out to Oleksandr Zinchenko at left-back and then straight across to Fernandinho. The positioning of those two players allows the ball to be played comfortably beyond the opposition player who is originally pressing the ball, and who was blocking the direct pass to Fernandinho.

The midfielder then has the time and space to identify and execute a pass through the inside of the opposition right-back for Leroy Sane to run on to and into the penalty area. Remember, we have already discussed in some detail that the priority for the City players is to find these passing lanes that allow the ball to be progressed beyond the defensive lines of the opposition.

By staggering their positioning and being on different lines to their team-mates, the ball can be progressed forward at each stage, creating more advantageous positions before the final pass can be played through and into an area that can be attacked.

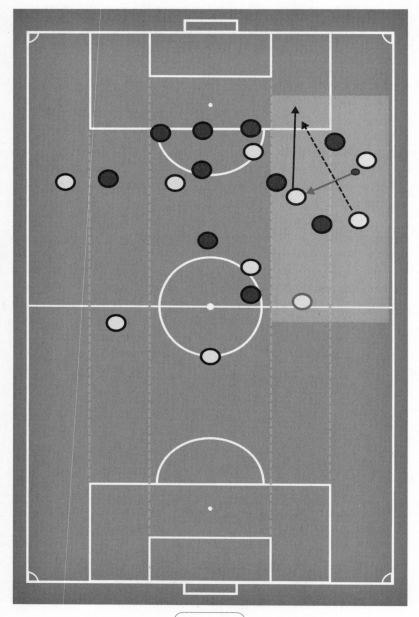

Figure 23

There are times with City in their attacking phase that one player in the overload can be disconnected from the rest of the attacking structure. In *figure 23*, for example, John Stones, on the right side of the centre-half pairing, is in position should the ball need to be moved back out of the final third. In advanced areas, City are positioned in a 3v3 structure on that side of the pitch, with Stones in a deeper area that becomes a 4v3.

Once again we see the slightly different lines that the three more advanced players have taken up. This depth is key as the ball is first moved back to Kevin De Bruyne, positioned in a more advanced area as the '8'. The position of De Bruyne and the right attacker, Riyad Mahrez, effectively pins the two closest defenders to them, creating a space in the defensive line that can be exploited. This space is used by Kyle Walker who makes a diagonal run at the same time as the pass is played into De Bruyne that allows him to break through and on to the vertical pass that De Bruyne is then free to play.

Once again we can see how important it is for City to ensure that they are positioned correctly in the attacking phase. At every stage the aim is to ensure that the ball can be played forward and to create angles that allow them to bypass the opposition as effectively as possible.

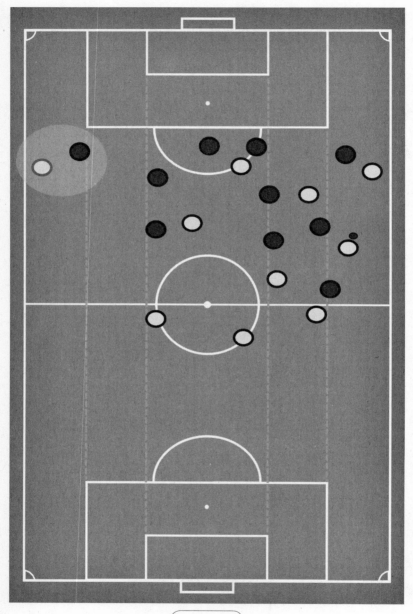

Figure 24

If City are unable to play through the overloaded side of the pitch then it is usually a direct result of the opposition shifting their defensive block across to block an opportunity for City to create passing lanes and pockets of space on the ball-near side of the pitch that they can take advantage of.

Figure 24 shows us a situation in which the opposition have shifted players across to the City right side. The two opposition players who were just entering the right-hand side half-space ended up moving across to block the possibility of the ball being played forward first to Raheem Sterling, wide on the right, and then into Bernardo Silva, who was playing on this occasion as the '8'. When this option is taken away we tend to see City first look to continue pulling the opponents over, through more short passes back and forth between two players. This completes the trap and City are then able to look to play across to the opposite side of the field where they have a wide attacker in isolation against a single defender.

This is why City always look to leave their wide attackers wide. The wide player on the ball-near side of the pitch is positioned to allow the '8' or the full-back to attack and occupy the half-space as the opposition full-back is committed wide to cover the attacker. On the opposite side of the pitch the wide player stays wide again but this time to force the defensive side to push at least one player across to cover them. This then allows City to pull the opposition across to one side before accessing the other side to finish the move.

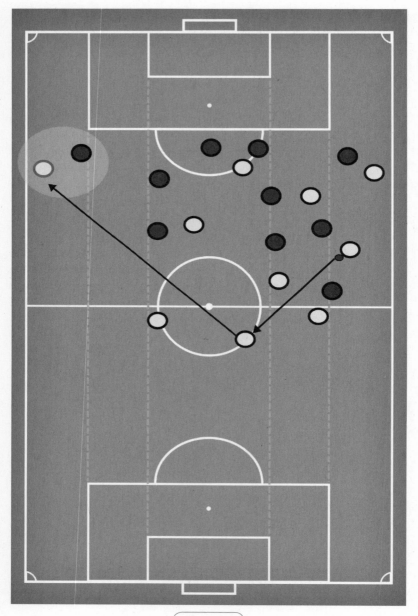

Figure 25

Even when looking to switch play, City still set out to ensure that they can retain possession. There are some instances in which the pass out to the opposite side is a single direct pass – when Kevin De Bruyne, with his exceptional passing range, is on the ball, for example. It is more common though for the pass out to the opposite side to travel across through another player.

We can see this in *figure 25,* where the aim for City is to play across to the left side where they have Leroy Sane isolated against a single defensive player. The ball is with Kyle Walker on the right side and he first shifts the ball backwards into Aymeric Laporte on the first line for City. On taking possession of the ball the central defender then has a clean line with which to access Sane out on the left-hand side.

In playing a pass back in this manner, City make sure that the switch of play is more secure. There is a slight risk that the opposition will be able to cover across to stop the isolated player from taking possession in a 1v1. The trick, however, is making sure that this pass back is part of a switch. If the opposition does over commit and shift across to cover the far side, then City will simply play back into the overloaded side to try to break through on that side.

As with so many things with City, it is one thing to know what they are trying to do, it is quite another to actually manage to stop them.

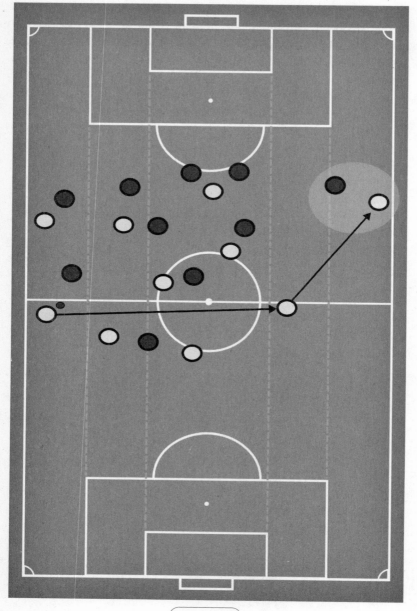

Figure 26

We can see a similar situation in *figure 26* with the ball and the overload on the left-hand side this time. The aim is the same as before; with the opposition flooding across to try to defend the overload, City want to switch over to where Raheem Sterling is isolated against a single defender.

Once again we see the ball switched over through a two-pass chain. The first ball goes from Aymeric Laporte, at left-back, through to Kyle Walker, at right-back. It can then be safely and securely moved out to Sterling on the right wing.

Under Pep Guardiola this Manchester City side are an attacking force to be reckoned with and the way that they create overloads is one of the central pieces of their success. Teams trying to defend and stop City from breaking through simply cannot defend the overload on one side and the isolated 1v1 on the opposite flank at the same time. Part of the genius of Guardiola is that he has developed a system that is balanced to the point that the attack can be focused down either side.

Chapter 5

Pressing

Over the last ten years or so the concept of pressing has become extremely fashionable in footballing circles. It is not that long ago that defensive actions were relatively passive with teams sitting in compact structures and waiting for the opposition to move into the final third. There were some teams and some individual players who would press, although they would do so in an isolated manner with little in the way of support. This began to change, as so much else in football did, when Pep Guardiola was in charge of Barcelona between 2008 and 2012. Not only were that Barcelona team strong in possession of the ball, they were also excellent without the ball, pressing and harrying the opposition into making mistakes in their own half before converting possession into goalscoring opportunities. Indeed, there were times that it seemed as though Barcelona had more players on the pitch than their opponents as they swarmed forward to press.

Early in his coaching career, Guardiola favoured a pressing structure that became widely known as the '5 second rule'. This rule dictated that when the side lost possession of the ball they would press ferociously for the first five seconds in order to regain possession of the ball. If they failed to do so in this time then they would drop into a more compact defensive shape to deny the opposition the space to play through or around them.

The thought behind this pressing structure was simple: Guardiola believed that the opposition were weakest in their possession phase when they initially regained the ball. The player who has won the ball will have expended energy in order to win the ball and will be slightly out of position in the first moments. To add to this, the opposition will not be structured in such a way to support the man in possession, having been dropping back to take up defensive positions when Barcelona were still in possession. With these two points in mind, Guardiola would have his side press with at least two or three players as soon as they lost the ball.

When Guardiola moved to Germany to coach Bayern Munich he came up against the big tactical trend in the country at the time of counter-pressing. Made famous by the high energy Borussia Dortmund side who were coached by Jurgen Klopp, counter-pressing took the '5-second rule' of Barcelona to the next level; in fact, Dortmund were a whirlwind of pressure when they lost the ball. Their relentless pressing style went far beyond just a few seconds with the entire team seeming to press aggressively when out of possession to prevent the opposition from having comfortable possession of the ball.

The exposure of Guardiola to this style of play when out of possession altered the way he thought about pressing. We never saw Bayern become a full counter-pressing side but they did alter their structure slightly in order to implement their own form of counter-press. When losing possession, Bayern would move to close potential passing lanes, forcing the opposition to play into an area of the field that had seemingly been left open. As the ball is played into this open space, the counter-press was triggered and Bayern would clamp down, looking to win the ball quickly.

What we see from Guardiola at City in terms of his pressing systems is something of an amalgamation of the two styles discussed above. He has learnt valuable lessons during his time at Barcelona and Bayern Munich and is now in a position to implement these lessons.

To this end we see Manchester City adopt a more flexible and reactive style to their pressing when out of possession, albeit with certain non-negotiables. When the opposition have the ball with their goalkeeper or with their central defenders, the normal action would be for the central forward to be the first to apply pressure. Instead, Guardiola prefers to use his two wide forwards to press centrally using curved runs. This enables them to press the ball while still preventing the pass out to the wide areas using their cover shadow. In the centre of the midfield, the two number '8's will press onto the midfielders of the opposition. The reactive side of the press comes in the use of the centre-forward and the full-backs. When City are pressing hard, the forward will also press the ball, trying to force a bad decision from the goalkeeper or the central defender in possession of the ball. The full-backs will also press higher in order to engage the opposition full-backs or wingers if the ball is played over the top of the initial press. The aim in the initial moments of pressure is to force the opposition to play into central areas where, as we already know, City will have looked to create numerical superiority over their opponents. As the play progresses and if the opposition are still in possession as they reach the City half of the field, then the priority shifts and City will look to close the central areas and force the opposition to play out in the wide spaces.

All of these movements take place over the course of just a few seconds. The first defensive action when out of possession for City tends to be to press. The only routine exceptions among the outfield players come in the two central defenders and the number '6', who tend to retain their defensive position, forming a triangle between them and making it difficult for the opposition to access the central areas with a quick and long pass.

That is not to say, however, that City are constantly looking to press and apply pressure. We see them drop back into a compact defensive block out of possession after the initial press if the opposition manages to retain possession. They will drop back to cut passing lanes and rest out of possession, but there is always a sense that they are ready to move back into a high press at any moment. These moments tend to come as soon as one of three pressing triggers are activated; If the opponent takes a poor touch and has to pause in possession; when the opposition pass the ball out to the wide area; and when the ball is played forward by the opposition to a player who is facing his own goal.

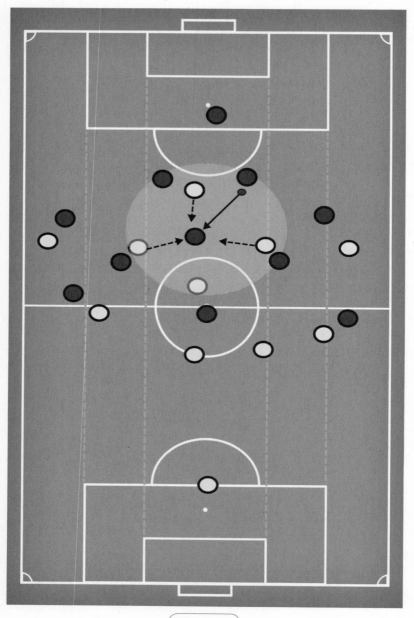

Figure 27

The first pressing trigger that we see used by Manchester City under Pep Guardiola is activated when the opposition player takes a poor touch on the ball. In *figure 27* we see the ball played by the opposition central defender into the player at the base of their midfield. As he receives the ball his first touch is poor and the ball bounces slightly away from his body.

This poor touch is enough to trigger a press from three City players as they look to engage on the poor touch. Sergio Aguero, the striker and David Silva and Ilkay Gundogan, the two '8's, all step towards the ball and look to constrict the space around the opposition player. With the opposition player having taken a poor touch they are immediately distracted. Instead of scanning for movements from the City players they will be fully focused on the ball as they attempt to bring it back under control. These split seconds as the opposition team player is distracted are key for the City players to close the space and ensure that they are engaging and pressuring the ball.

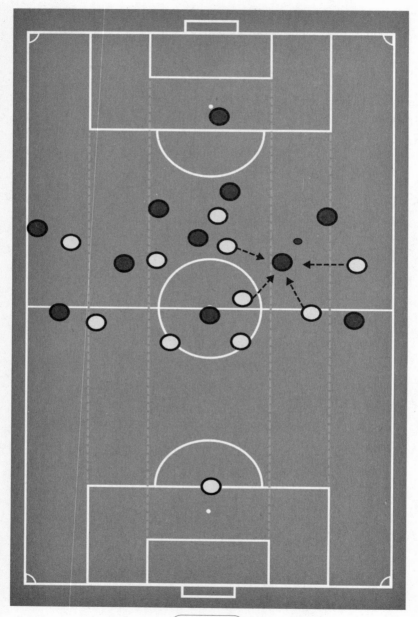

Figure 28

Figure 28 again shows a similar example with the opposing team looking to build from a defensive position and progress the ball forward. As the ball comes forward the man looking to receive the ball takes a loose touch back towards the man who had played the original pass.

This touch once again acts as the trigger for the press, with four players moving from their positions to converge on the ball. The man who has taken the poor touch can of course regain the ball and play the ball backwards, but at this point the pressing movement has already started. City would then press the pass backwards in order to close the space that the defensive player has to play in.

The initial poor touch set off the chain reaction that led to City being able to regain possession, through a poor pass forward from the defensive player after the ball had been played back into him.

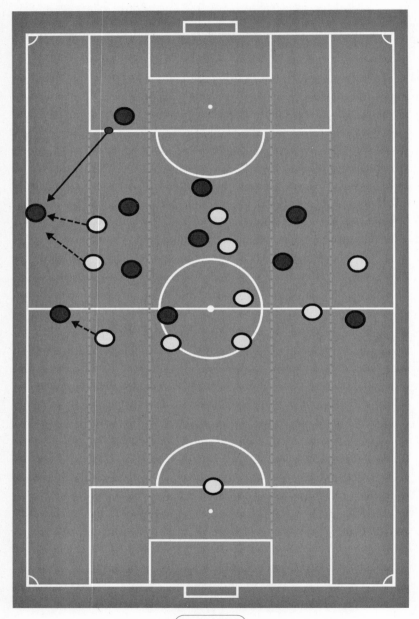

Figure 29

The second pressing trigger that we see used by City to decide when they will engage the ball comes when the ball is passed out to the wide area. This trigger is easy to understand and is based on the reduced area of movement that a player has when they take possession in that area. With the touchline to one side, the player with the ball only has the scope to play in 180 degrees with their options limited.

This means that as the ball is played into the wide area, City will move to engage the ball quickly. We can see an example of this in *figure 29* as the ball is played forward from the goalkeeper to the full-back out in the wide space. There are two City players who immediately press and engage the ball as it is played out into the wide zone. The key, however, comes in the angle of the run made by the pressing player. One City player moves towards the ball at an angle but does so in such a way that he is cutting off a passing lane that would allow the full-back to take the ball and pass back inside towards the central defender. These angled runs prevent the opponents from escaping easily once the press is triggered.

We also see a third City player who is activated by the pass out to the wide space. The left-back for City moves across tighter to engage with the advanced player for the opposition on the ball side of the pitch. This prevents the man who takes the ball in the right-back area from having an easy pass forward that would allow him to escape the pressure.

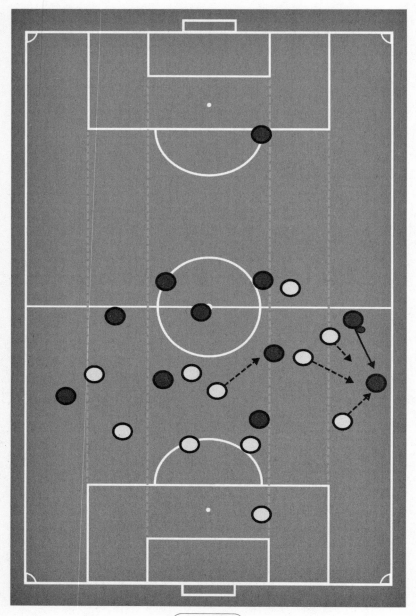

Figure 30

The same concept can be seen in *figure 30* as the opposition play into the wide area in a more advanced part of the pitch.

The rules behind the pressing trigger remain the same. As the ball is moved out to the wide player who is on an advanced line, the three closest City players move in to engage the ball and prevent the man taking possession from having time to think and play. Once again there is a player who positions himself and angles his run to press the ball while preventing the ball from being played centrally.

Again, we also see a City player moving out of the structure beyond the immediate press in order to be closely positioned beside the central opponent as an extra measure to stop the ball from being played into central areas.

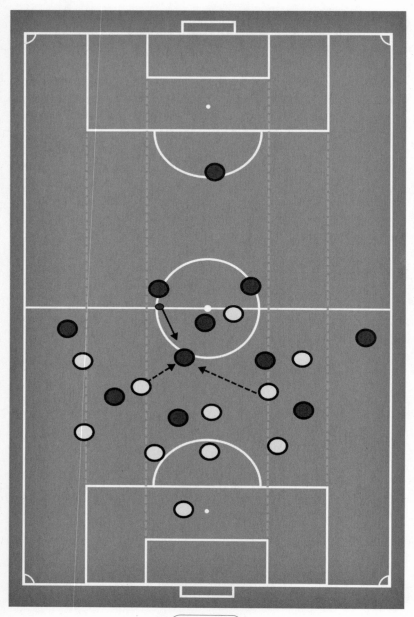

Figure 31

The final trigger that we see City utilise within their pressing structure is set when the pass is played forward by the opposition to a player who is facing his own goal when he receives the ball. Once again there is nothing overly complicated about this concept. A player who is facing his own goal when taking possession of the ball is less aware of the picture behind him or of the positions of his own team-mates or the City players.

Figure 31 sees this concept in action. As the ball is played forward by the opposition into a central area, the player who is receiving the ball is facing his own goal and had not scanned over his shoulder prior to the pass being made. As the ball is played into the opposition player in the midfield area, we see two City players moving to converge on the ball in order to create an opportunity for a turnover.

It is situations such as this which showcase the importance of players scanning, whether they are in or out of possession. This is the simple process of moving your head to scan your surrounding area as often as possible. This allows a player to build a mental image of not only the position of other players on the pitch but also where there is space that could be used. The process of scanning and developing a picture of the pitch is often what separates great players from those who are merely good.

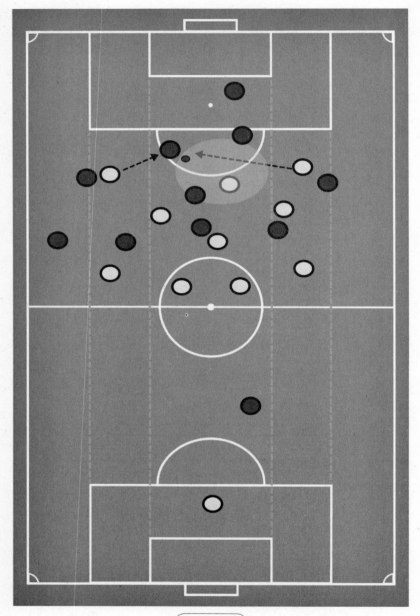

Figure 32

Often when the opposition are looking to play out initially we will see City press the ball initially with their two wide forwards. You can see this in *figure 32* as Raheem Sterling, from the right, and Leroy Sane, from the left, move inside in order to close down and engage the ball.

These movements prevent the opposition from playing from central areas out to the wide zones in order to potentially bypass the press from City and play into advanced areas. As the wide players move in and press, the central striker is able to drop off slightly, both as an opportunity to rest briefly while out of possession and to be ready to move and press should the ball be played forward into central areas.

As the ball is played forward centrally, with the two wide players having moved and closed down the ball initially out of position, the onus is on the two '8's to be able to press forward to support the striker should the pass be made out of the pressure.

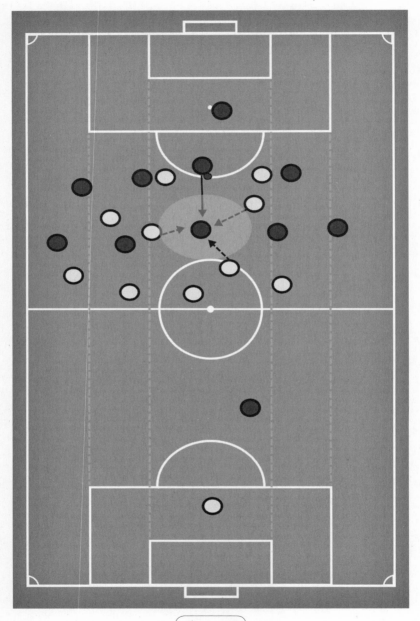

Figure 33

There is little point in creating and adapting pressing traps and triggers to prevent your opposition from playing through your defensive structure easily if you allow them to escape the press easily. This is why we see City players position themselves in such a way as to block easy passing lanes that would allow the opposition to dictate the direction of play. The idea is for City to block passing lanes into areas that they do not want their opponents to play into, while also leaving what looks like a clear passing lane that the other side will look to use.

Figure 33 shows this, as the opposition has the ball with a central defender. The option to play out to the left or the right is taken away as City players are blocking the passing lanes that would allow the other team to access these areas. The option is still on for the opposing central defender to play forwards. As he does so, however, he triggers the trap and three City players are able to move out and press the ball.

Pressing is essential in the modern game. Manchester City, under Pep Guardiola, are exceptional when in possession of the ball. They dominate games and mesmerise their opponents with passing combinations that pull the opposition out of position time and time again. City cannot achieve this attacking dominance, however, without the ball, so they have strictly implemented pressing triggers that tell the players when and how to engage the ball in order to achieve the highest chance of creating a turnover and winning the ball back. City are by no means though a side which press all of the time or that press without a plan or structure. Instead everything is thought out and planned on the training field before being implemented in a match situation.

Chapter 6

Cutting Passing Lanes and Defensive Compactness

While we have already considered the manner in which Manchester City press the opposition when they are out of possession, and the triggers that lead to that press, this is not the only defensive concept that we have to examine. Although City dominate possession of the ball in almost every match that they play, there is still a need at times for them to drop back into a more compact defensive shape. This requires the players on the pitch to have an understanding of how to form a compact block and how to prevent the opposition from finding passing lanes to play through the City defensive block. Given that the use and exploitation of these passing lanes is a key aspect of City's attacking game plan, they should all recognise the importance of defending these.

The term 'passing lanes' is one that is used to describe a simple concept. They refer to a channel or 'lane' that exists between defensive players and through which the ball can be played via a pass. The slightly more complex aspect of these lanes is that they are ever shifting. You may be in possession of the ball in the half-space with a passing lane ahead of you that will release a team-mate behind the defensive line. In the space of just a few seconds this lane can be closed by a defensive player shifting slightly over to one side or another. The key, when attacking, is to understand that when a defensive player shifts to block a passing lane, they potentially leave another one open in the space that they have just vacated. This translates over to the way that City try to deny the opposition this kind of space in their defensive phase.

In order to prevent these lanes from opening up, City will look to retain a high level of defensive compactness. As we have already seen, they will look to press, if the situation and the triggers allow, but this is only the case up to a point. Once the opposition have regained position and are in an established attacking phase, we see City drop deeper to defend in a shape that approaches a 4-5-1 – for all that formations matter! – with only the forward player left in an advanced position. This compactness has two main aims for Pep Guardiola. The first is to allow his players to rest out of possession. Typically, City are dynamic and explosive in the attacking phase; this means that when they get a chance to drop to a deep or medium defensive block they will use this time to regain their energy. They will still need to shift left and right in order to prevent overloads but they can do so while conserving effort. The second reason for this compactness is to ensure that each City player has defensive support. This means that as the opposition attack a section of the City block they will not find a single player that can be isolated without support. This close connection between defensive players also means that when a pressing trigger is activated in the defensive third of the field, then there are two or three, at minimum, City players who will be able to collapse on the ball in order to create a turnover.

We also have to consider the more simple reason for City to employ defensive compactness in this manner: to make it difficult for the opposition players to play through and threaten the penalty area as they try to move into advanced positions. In order to play effectively through a compact block you have to have creative players who are capable of finding the pockets of space that are left open in the opposition defensive block. This is something that we see City largely excel at in the attacking phase with the two '8's within the tactical system in particular being exceptional when it comes to identifying and occupying these spaces. When City are sitting in their defensive block we see Fernandinho, as the '6', fill an important function as he denies the opposition access to pockets of space in between the lines.

This defensive compactness is also, of course, a function that Guardiola will use in order to exert control over spaces that the opposition are looking to dominate themselves. If the defensive structure for City was more spread out and less compact, then the opportunity would be there for the opposition to create numerical overloads in key areas that would allow them to break through. This is particularly true when it comes to the central areas of the field, a key tactical battleground, and one that Guardiola will look to defend at all costs. If City were spread out and not compact then the other side would be able to occupy these areas with a view to creating scoring opportunities. Instead, City remain compact and only allow space in the wide areas for the opposition to attack.

There is simply no way that any defensive side would be able to cover all areas of their own half equally. As with in the attacking phase, we see City implement their defensive block with three key references. This time, though, the priority is as follows: firstly, the ball, secondly, the opposition, and thirdly, their own team-mates. The defensive block is then set to ensure that the ball cannot be played easily through and that the opposition are not able to find space in which to occupy. This tends to mean that the City block remains relatively central and of course the opposition can access the wide areas in an attempt to play around the block. These situations, however, usually see City then rotate across quickly to press the ball in the wide areas. There is simply no easy way for opponents to break through the block.

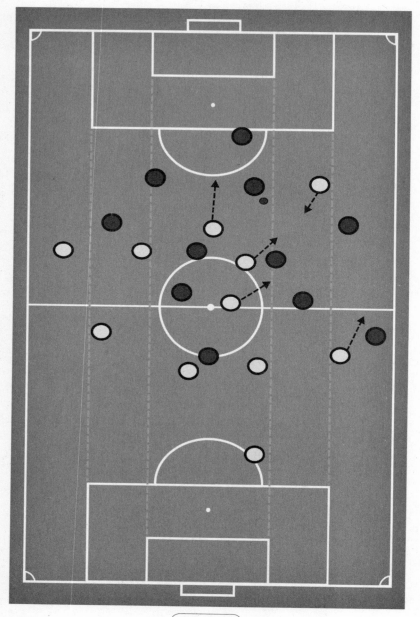

Figure 34

First of all we should consider the way that City move and rotate in order to cut passing lanes in the initial moments after they lose possession or as the opposition look to build out from the back. These rotations are designed to prevent the man in possession from finding easy passes that they can use in order to progress the ball forwards into the central areas of the field. The first reaction from City is to block these passing lanes, and the second is to then press the ball while also using angles of approach and body shape to continue to block these lanes. The whole process can take just seconds so the coordination and understanding of the City players has to be perfect.

We see these rotations in action in *figure 34* as the opposition central defender is in possession of the ball deep inside his own half. The two players that are closest to the ball move quickly to prevent the ball being progressed either centrally or out to the opposition's left-hand side. We then see similar movements from three more City players who move to position themselves in the open passing lanes for the man in possession.

All of this is designed to limit the options that are open to the man in possession and to force him to make a difficult choice. Does he try to access one of these passing lanes anyway? Does he hit the longer pass hoping for a mistake from the City defender? Or does he play back to the goalkeeper? If the ball is hit long or goes back to the goalkeeper then City will be immediately triggered into a pressing action in order to regain possession. If he tries to play into the passing lanes then City have a good chance of winning back possession. Simple but effective.

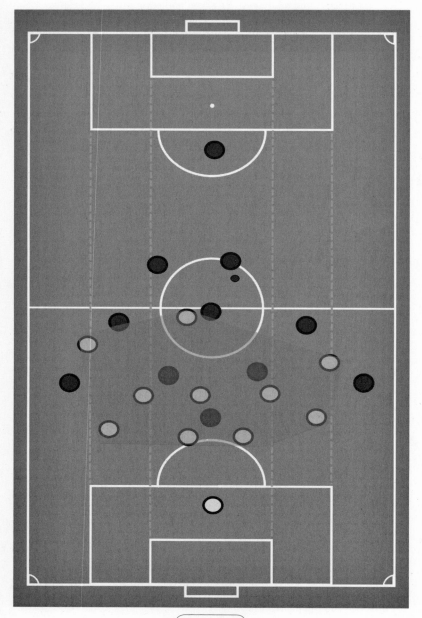

Figure 35

The defensive compactness that we see from City when they drop into deeper areas is meant to ensure that each defensive player is closely supported by a team-mate. You can see an example of this defensive shape and structure in *figure 35*. The opposition defender is in possession just inside his own half. City have dropped into a 4-5-1 structure with the emphasis remaining on defending the centre of the pitch.

As you can see, the block only reaches so far across the field with the central areas covered completely. The opposition have space to progress the ball in wide areas if they are quick enough to feed the ball into these areas. The trick for the opposition is managing to access these areas without City then closing a pressing trap in order to close the space and turn over possession. The entire City structure will shift left and right in order to maintain the spacing between the defensive players and prevent the opposition from finding space that they can exploit centrally.

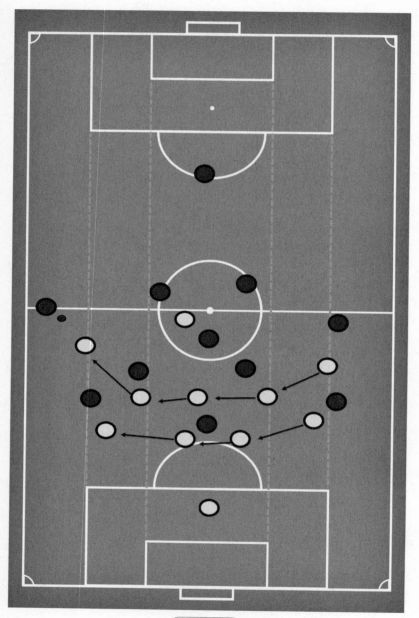

Figure 36

In order to be able to shift across from left to right and back again to close space ahead of the opposition, every player needs to be engaged and understand his role. As with many good football sides, City understand this concept well and execute the movements across to close down space.

We can see how this concept works in *figure 36* with the opposition in possession of the ball wide on the right-hand side. Once again the general defensive structure that we see from City sees four defenders and five midfielders in a chain with a lone forward ahead of them. As the ball is in the wide areas, the players in the defensive structure flow across as shown in the image.

The aim is for the man in possession to be trapped on one side of the field with no space to play forward, either to the wide areas or into the centre of the pitch. If the opposition are then able to escape this pressure, usually by playing back and then out to the opposite side, then the process reverses and City would shift across in the opposite direction in order to close down that side of the field. The key is for each player to have to move only a short distance to either side. This prevents the City players from expending too much energy and ensures that when they do regain possession they are in a position to transition quickly into their attacking phase.

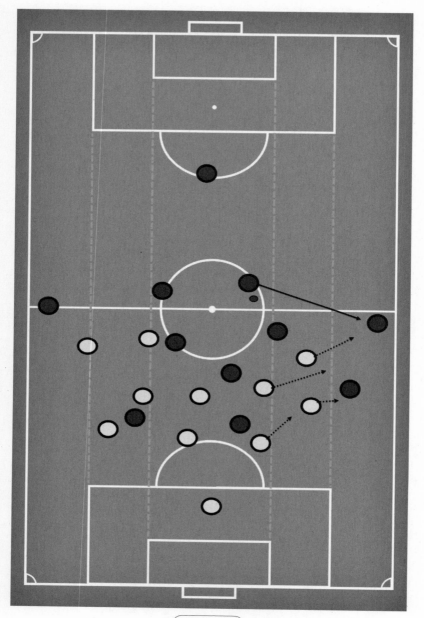

Figure 37

As the opposition look to escape the defensive block we will often see them recycle the ball back to the first line, the defenders, before looking to play out again to the opposite side of the field from the initial attack. If they are able to play these passes with enough speed then it is possible that they will be able to break through the City block in the wide areas.

What we tend to see is that as the opposition speed up the tempo with a direct pass that is played quickly out to the wide spaces, then City will immediately press that pass with numbers in order to prevent a breakthrough.

This press has two key aims: first of all to regain possession if at all possible, and the pass out to the wide area does represent one of the pressing triggers that we tend to see from City. Secondly, to force the opposition to stall their attacking movement as this will allow City the time to rotate their block across as we have seen previously.

Figure 37 shows this in action as the opposition central defender has played the ball from the central area out to the left-hand side we immediately see four City players shift across to engage the ball and slow down the progress of the attack.

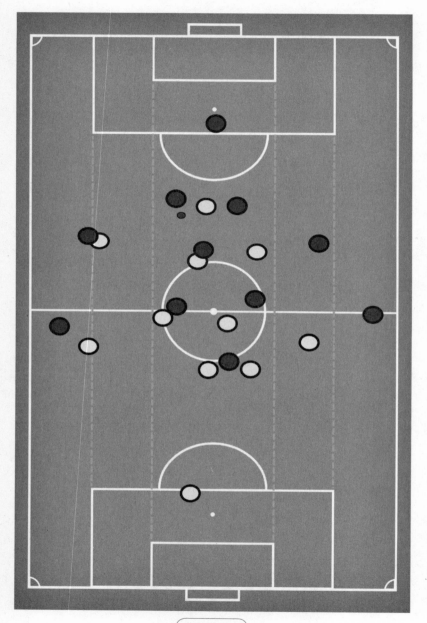

Figure 38

There are times when the opposition have possession of the ball in their own half that we see City altering their defensive shape slightly in order to almost challenge man to man. This is obviously a risky strategy because all that it takes is for the opposition to beat one City player and the defensive structure is under pressure.

The City forward player will split the two defenders for the opposition to prevent them from playing the ball between them to change the angle of the attack. Ahead of the ball, City press up against the opposition and prevent any opportunity for the ball to be played into the advanced areas. Once again the aim is to force the opposition player in possession to try to force a pass forward into an area which can be attacked by the City defenders.

We see these movements and press in action in *figure 38* as City have essentially taken away any options that the opposition have to play into advanced areas.

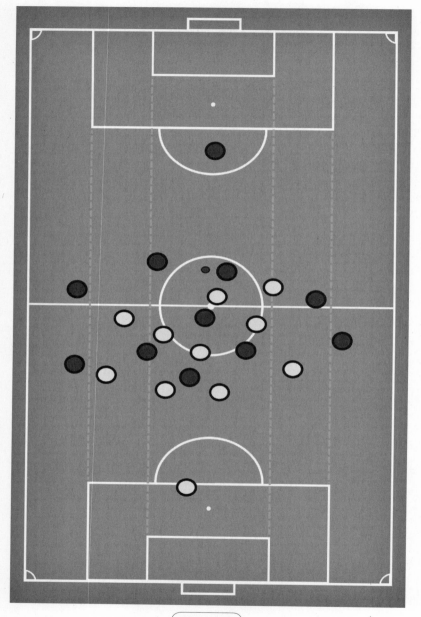

Figure 39

This man-to-man marking structure is used both as a tool to try to win back possession and as a means for City to delay the attacking movement for long enough to allow them to drop back into a compact block.

As the attacking move that we saw above is delayed and the opposition go backwards before trying to move forward once again, we see City drop into their compact shape. The key is to prevent the opposition from finding the pockets of space that can prove dangerous to the City penalty area.

We see this in *figure 39* as the opposition again has the ball with their central defender. The pass out to the left for the man in possession is blocked because the City wide attacker has blocked the passing lane. The ball can be circulated over to the other central defender but you can already see that there are no passing lanes ahead of that player which would allow the ball to be played into advanced areas. Even if the ball is then played out again to the right-hand side there will be no easy pass to allow the ball to be progressed. The trap is then tightened further as the ball travels across and the City forward keeps cutting the passing lane that would allow the ball to be played back inside. Once again the opposition will have to play a pass into pressure or go back to their goalkeeper, losing any advantage they might have had.

When we consider Manchester City under Pep Guardiola, we do not necessarily think about defensive concepts. In football today, however, it is not enough for a top level coach to be strong in the attacking phase or in the defensive phase. Instead they have to be able to do both equally well. There is no doubt that Guardiola understands space on the football pitch in a way that few others do or ever have. The genius of the Spaniard is that he is able to apply this understanding to when his side do not have the ball as well as when they do have the ball. This part of the Manchester City game model is often overlooked.

Chapter 7

'8's as '10's

Football at its heart is a sport of romance and history. Great players and great teams are held in reverence, with the narrative around them only growing as the years pass and people remembering the good while forgetting the bad. Such is the romanticism surrounding the game, this nostalgia extends to something as obscure as shirt numbers. Shirt numbers have over the years become irrevocably connected with types of players, with no number perhaps being held in more high regard than the number '10'.

The number '10' in football terms is thought of as an attacking playmaker, a player who operates in the hole between the lines of midfield and attack. These players are, typically, highly creative types who possess the kind of control and skill that can entertain and inspire fans.

When you think about the best number '10's that have played over the years, the names will come thick and fast, in no particular order: Roberto Baggio, Francesco Totti, Zinedine Zidane... the list could go on and on. Iconic players wearing iconic shirts.

It could be argued, however, that modern football has moved away from the traditional number '10'. The rise in prominence of tactical structures like the 4-3-3, popularised hugely by the Barcelona of Pep Guardiola, has seen teams use the normalised structure of a number '6', at the base of the midfield, and two number '8's in more advanced positions.

Over the last decade or so within top level football we have seen a clear preference for teams to utilise the midfield structure that we see above. There are some teams who alter things slightly and play with two number '6's as a double pivot at the base of the midfield.

This perhaps more defensively solid solution in the midfield would be unthinkable to Guardiola, who played for his entire career as the number '6' in single pivot systems.

While he was still a young player, Guardiola learnt the tactical side of football from the legendary Dutch coach Johan Cruyff, and the Dutchman was convinced that playing with a single pivot allows for better ball progression than playing with two players as '6's.

We have seen some slight variations from City, particularly in the 2018/19 season, with the match at home to Arsenal seeing Fernandinho, normally the sole '6', playing on the defensive line. When City were in possession, the Brazilian would rotate into the midfield to the same line as Ilkay Gundogan. This allowed City to progress the ball comfortably past the Arsenal press and showed that Guardiola is more of a flexible tactician than many had thought.

More often than not, however, we see City using the former structure. The problem facing Guardiola when he came to Manchester City in 2016 was that he possessed a player with all of the hallmarks of a classic number '10', David Silva. Looking back, it seems absurd that there could be any question surrounding the place of Silva in a Guardiola team, given he has shown himself to be the key player in both understanding and implementing Pep's game model. In order to achieve this, though, the City boss first had to find a way to unlock the creative potential of Silva, amongst others, to play further forward from the number '8' position.

He did something that was, in retrospect, extremely simple. He instructed his two number '8's, typically Silva and Kevin De Bruyne, to play much further forward in positions that are more typically occupied by number '10's. This positional concept was achievable at City because Guardiola has complete trust in those who play in deeper positions to be able to progress the ball forward without relying on the two central midfielders. The triangle formed by the two central defenders and Fernandinho, as the single pivot, gives City an exceptional base from which they can build their attacks. They also have full-backs who are capable of occupying wide areas or moving into more narrow positions as the situation requires. All of this allows the likes of Silva and De Bruyne the freedom to operate in higher areas.

The key to the positioning of the two number '8's is that they occupy spaces in the field known as the half-spaces. The half-space is a term that has become increasingly popularised in terms of football analysis. It simply refers to two vertical lanes on the pitch.

As we split a football pitch vertically to create 5 lanes then the half-spaces refer to lanes 2 and 4. The importance of these zones comes from the flexibility in terms of movement and passing that players have when occupying these zones. In the wide areas the range of movements of a player in position is limited by the touchline to one side, while the central areas are often congested and tight. The half-spaces offer space and time for attacking players to receive the ball before attacking the opposition defensive structure. It is here that we see the two more advanced midfielders position themselves to maximise the attacking potential of the City tactical system.

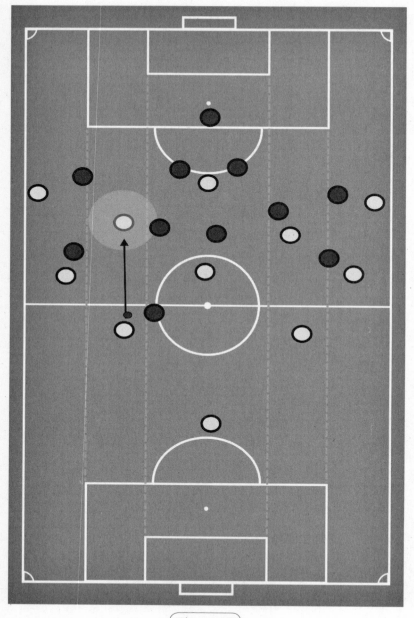

Figure 40

When Manchester City have possession of the ball, the two number '8's take up an extremely high line, often level with or just behind the two wide forwards, and they position themselves firmly within the half-spaces. This creates a split within the City structure when they initially start to build up towards the final third, of 5-5. The two central defenders, the number '6' and the full-backs form the first 5 while the two '8's, the wide forwards and the lone striker make the second 5.

As the attacking play develops, the two units are joined together, usually by the two full-backs or even the '6' moving to a higher line. This movement within the attacking phase creates connections and passing angles across the width and depth of the pitch that allow City to circulate the ball extremely effectively.

The positioning of the two '8's for City in the half-spaces becomes extremely important as they move the ball forward. They are often positioned in pockets of space either between the opposition midfielders or behind them. From these areas, when these attacking players receive the ball, they can disrupt the opposition defensive organisation and force overloads against isolated defensive players.

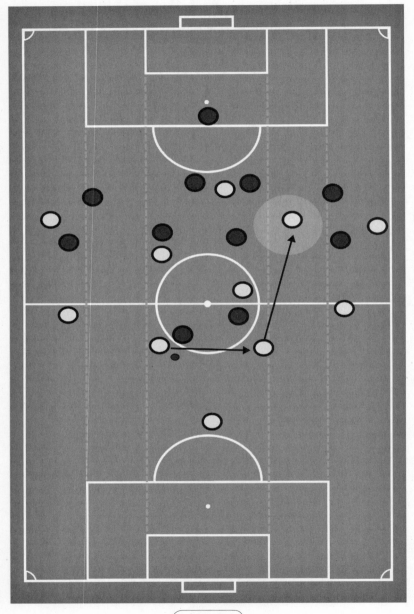

Figure 41

As you can see in *figure 41* the key is in the positioning of the '8' in space. The opposition were pressing City in a 4-4-2 with the two forward players applying heavy pressure in order to prevent the City central defenders from playing out comfortably. It is in these areas that we see how comfortable Pep Guardiola's side truly are in possession of the ball. The first pass goes to the second central defender; this bypasses the press, at least until the opposition forward can adjust, and gives City the vertical passing lane that they need to play into the feet of Kevin De Bruyne, who is on a high line in the half-space.

Quite often we will see the two '8's for City take up different lines on the pitch with one dropping deeper towards the ball and one staying higher. This prevents the opposition from comfortably setting up in a defensive structure that can negate the two central players for City.

The kind of short directional passing that we see in the first pass above is a common tactical concept used by City. Some feel that they often pass the ball for passing's sake with these short passes, but in truth these passes have two intentions. The first is to tempt the opposition to move from their defensive positions in order to put pressure on the ball; if this happens then City will exploit the space left in the defensive structure with ruthless efficiency. The second intention is to move the ball into a player who has a vertical passing option as we see above. The player in possession of the ball initially is blocked by the opposition press from playing forwards. By playing the simple sideways pass, the player receiving possession is able to play forwards to access the final third in a single pass.

When the players on the defensive line are in possession of the ball it is common to see one of the two '8's dropping into deeper areas in order to give a passing option and allow for the ball to be progressed forward. When they do so they will always stay in the half-space and give the option between the central defender and full-back.

Figure 42

There are subtle differences in terms of how the two '8's operate when helping to progress the ball from deep areas, each of which deserves some explaining. In *Figure 42* we see a situation where City are struggling to easily progress the ball against an opponent who is pressing in a 4-1-4-1 shape. David Silva, positioned on the left of the midfield three, drops back to ease the ball progression but in doing so he effectively creates a chain of three defenders across the first line. As he drops into this position the left-back or the '6' will generally rotate over to fill the space that he has vacated to give Silva an option for passing the ball forwards. Again we have to return to the two intentions, or principles, that we discussed above. The first pass into the central area does not give the man taking possession the option of playing vertically. The second pass, made possible by the movement of Silva, does allow this vertical pass to be played.

As soon as City are able to play vertically they bypass layers of the opposition press and start to create opportunities in and around the final third.

Figure 43

Figure 43 shows the second type of movement that we see towards the ball. As the central defender is in possession, the opposition are pressing with three forward players effectively covering the passing options that City would normally use to progress the ball. This time David Silva drops not into the defensive line but to the same line as the '6', which creates the double pivot that we spoke about earlier in the chapter. The double pivot is a concept that is not used regularly by City under Pep Guardiola but that is formed when the need arises. In this example, Silva is able to receive the vertical pass in space before turning and driving forward with the ball.

The positioning of the two '8's for City in the half-spaces, where they can exploit space in and around the opposition midfield, can at times force an extreme reaction from the other team as they look to deny the space that the two City advanced midfielders can exploit. This comes when the midfield unit for the other side collapses back in order to form a compact unit behind the positions that City will generally build from. When this happens, it is no surprise that Guardiola has the solution ready to implement.

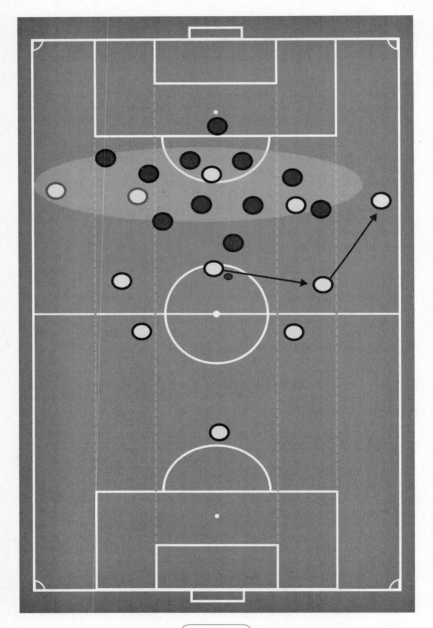

Figure 44

In *figure 44* we see the opposition defending in an extremely compact 4-4-2 system. Even with the '6' in possession of the ball in the opposition half there is still limited pressure being applied to the ball. The opposition in the above example are intent on preventing City from attacking in the central areas of the field, with no easy pass into either of the two '8's. Instead the wide forwards and full-backs become key to progressing the ball.

The two full-backs will move in towards the half-spaces and take up positions on the same line as the '6'. The two wide forwards will, as always, take up an extremely high line and hold a very wide position. City can comfortably progress the ball through the full-backs and out to the wide forwards. It is when the ball reaches these wide areas that we will see a reaction from the opposition defensive structure. As the ball moves out wide, the opposition have to decide whether to allow the City wide attackers to have possession in these high areas, dangerous given the quality they have in these areas, or whether to engage and press the ball.

If they press the ball then once again the '8's will come alive with space vacated in and around the opposition defensive structure, so they will be able to access these spaces and play in combination with the wide players.

On each side of the field the '8's for City are effective in the attacking phase when they can combine with the wide players. Indeed, they are equally effective in combining with the lone forward. It is now that we can begin to fully understand just how integral these two players are to everything that Pep Guardiola wants to do in the final third of the pitch, and the positioning of the two players in the half-spaces is key to this.

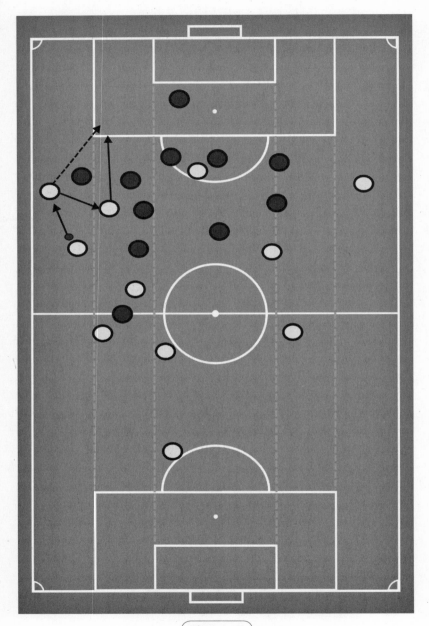

Figure 45

In *figure 45* we see City in possession of the ball with the left-back looking to progress the ball down the wide area. David Silva is positioned just inside the wide forward, just on the line of the half-space and the wide area.

With the opposition seeking to deny City the space to play into central areas, as we can see from the positioning of their players denying the central passing lanes, they have the potential for a 3v1 overload in the wide area. The pass is initially played into the wide forward, and this pass pins the opposition defender in position and effectively prevents him from splitting the wide forward and Silva by positioning himself between the two. With the ball going wide he cannot take the risk of backing off.

The key comes with the next pass and the quick combination that isolates and overloads the defender. As the ball is quickly shifted inside to Silva then the defender has to react. As he starts to shift position, the wide forward is already moving on a diagonal line beyond the ball, and the overload is complete when Silva plays the return pass into the path of the wide forward.

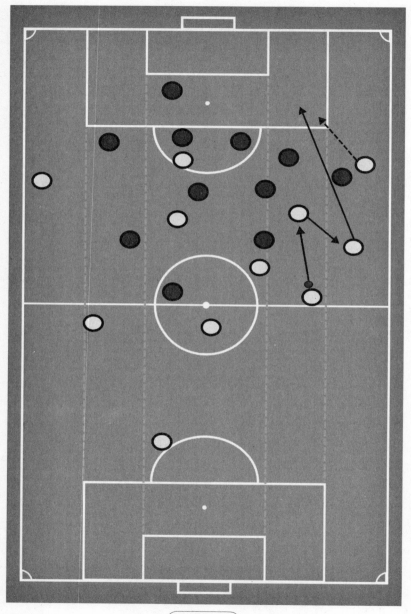

Figure 46

The same kind of pass can be made in *figure 46* as City progress the ball down the right side of the field, this time through Kevin De Bruyne through the right half-space. As the ball is played forward initially into De Bruyne he has the ability to play back to the full-back who is unmarked. The first priority for City under Pep Guardiola will be, as we discussed earlier in the chapter, to play the pass vertically through the lines of the opposition. As soon as the ball is played into whoever is playing as the '8'in these positions you will see the wide forward, or the full-back if they are high enough, start to make the diagonal run beyond the defensive line. They trust completely the technical ability and the vision of the '8's within the squad not only to see the run but also to be able to execute the pass to get the ball through.

The two '8's who operate within this 4-3-3 under Guardiola present a new type of midfielder. They have the ability to press and defend passing lanes in the defensive phase but in the attacking phase they come alive. Whether dropping to help progress the ball or holding a high line to receive possession in space, they operate with the vision and freedom of expression that used to be reserved for the true '10's that were discussed in the opening of this chapter. What is perhaps more impressive is that it does not seem to matter which players occupy these spaces. David Silva, De Bruyne, Bernardo Silva, Ilkay Gundogan and Phil Foden have all received significant minutes as the '8's over the course of two seasons for City, and all of these players have different playing styles. All that this seems to do is offer a sense of variety in the way that City move the ball in the final third.

Chapter 8
Kyle Walker

At the end of his first season in charge, a season where by his own high standards his side had underperformed, Pep Guardiola was aware that there was a need to refresh and reshape his first-team squad. Looking back from where we are now, after two successive titles and a domestic treble in his most recent season in charge, there are people around football keen to point out that Guardiola has enjoyed the benefits of enormous spending. Those points are, of course, understandable when viewed in isolation but what is often overlooked is just how targeted and successful the recruitment at City under Guardiola has been.

Going into his second full season in charge, Guardiola and his staff were obviously aware that the output from their full-backs over the course of the 2016/17 season had been sorely lacking. Originally there were reports that Guardiola wanted to add right-back Dani Alves, who played under Pep at Barcelona, to the squad.

The Brazilian, however, rejected the offer and elected to move to Paris St Germain instead. Despite this setback,

City moved quickly and decisively to sign the Tottenham and England right-back Kyle Walker instead.

Originally a product of the youth set-up at Sheffield United, Walker had firmly established himself as the first-choice right-back for club and country. His career progression to that point, however, was not as linear as many are in his position.

When Walker made the breakthrough at first-team level with United he only played twice before agreeing a move to Spurs, along with his fellow academy graduate Kyle Naughton. At the time of signing, there was still some doubt as to whether Walker would develop as a right-back or as a left-back, such was the versatility that he displayed. This versatility would prove an interesting insight into the way that Walker would be used by Guardiola at City.

As a Spurs player, Walker had to wait to make his impact in the first team. As a part of the deal that took him to London, he was loaned back to Sheffield United for the whole of the following season. This period at least allowed the youngster to establish himself in the professional game, although this was only the first loan season that Walker faced as he moved to Queens Park Rangers and then Aston Villa on loan for the next two seasons. Finally, after three full seasons out on loan, he was given his chance to state a claim for a first-team role at Spurs.

Gradually over the course of that season, Walker earned his place. As a younger player, he always possessed top level pace but now he added extra muscle that allowed him to stand up to the physical demands of the Premier League. Gradually we also started to see the other elements of his game begin to improve and grow. He became more positionally aware in both in the attacking and defensive phases of the game, displaying a more nuanced ability to read the game and take positions that were advantageous to his team. Perhaps just as importantly we began to see Walker improve his decision making and technical delivery in the final third. While previously his pace and power would allow him to access space in behind the opposition defensive line, now he had the ability to fully capitalise on these positions with an understanding of how and when to make the final pass.

It should come as no surprise that Manchester City tracked Walker and invested a significant sum, a reported £53m, in securing his signature. He possessed the dynamic qualities that Guardiola favoured in his full-backs and had already shown versatility and a willingness to learn new roles within his team. It also did not hurt that as an English international, the signing of Walker would benefit City under the rules for squad registration in the Premier League, where currently there is a home-grown player rule which states that at least eight players in the 25-man squad have to have been on the books of an English club for at least three years before they turn 21.

So far, Walker's career at City has been an unqualified success. He is the perfect full-back for Guardiola with the athletic ability and technical quality to create overlaps around the outside, and underlaps on the inside, of the wide players when they are in possession of the ball. We have also seen two slightly different roles in which Walker has been used during his City career. In possession, at times, City play effectively with three centre-backs. The left-back will advance to an advanced line and Walker will retain a deeper line forming a chain of three with the other two defenders. Secondly, we have seen Walker used in an inverted full-back role. This was a role that we saw Guardiola use extensively while at Bayern Munich where he would use his two full-backs, David Alaba and Philipp Lahm, to move infield in possession almost as extra central midfielders. In matches where the opposition sits in a deep and passive defensive block, we have seen Guardiola choose to do similar with Walker, with the England international moving infield to play on the same line as the '6' in the City system.

That Walker is considered by Guardiola to have the technical and tactical capacity to fill these varied roles for this City side is testament to how highly the right-back is thought of by his coach. It also shows once again that Guardiola is capable of continually improving his players. Walker came to City as a top class full-back with a physical profile that fits the modern game. There are few amongst us who would have looked at Walker and seen that he would be capable of playing in possession as a central midfielder. Guardiola, however, did see this and he set about developing Walker and ensuring that the player had all of the tactical information that he would require to fill that role and fill it well.

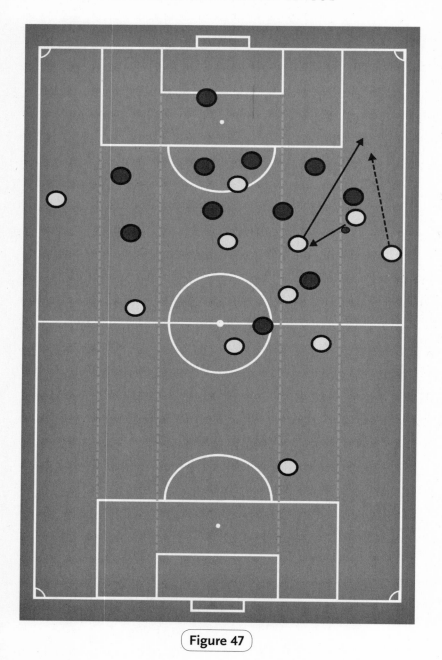

Figure 47

We have already seen in a previous chapter that Pep Guardiola places a large amount of importance on the role played by the full-backs. They are expected to fulfil three, or four, different functions within that system. Here is the thing, though: the way that each full-back interprets this role will change depending on that player's individual identity.

A player's identity in footballing terms is naturally unique to them. You can take two players who play the same position in the same team with the same instructions from the coach but the way that they play on the field will differ depending on their traits. Take Kyle Walker and Danilo, for example. Both have been used as right-back within this system but while Danilo is more likely to either retain a deep position, in support of the ball, or move up the wide spaces when they are empty, Walker is far more nuanced in his movements.

The first thing that we need to recognise is just how effective Walker is when he advances forward in the wide areas. We see an example of this in *figure 47*. As the ball is moved back from the wide player to the '8', who has occupied the half-space, the defensive players for the opposition are fixated on the position of the ball, and the space wide on the right is open. This space effectively releases Walker who makes a run outside, on the blind side of the nearest opponent, and creates the passing angle for the player in possession of the ball to play diagonally in order to release him.

With the physical traits of Walker, his pace and his power, the key for him in this City system is understanding when and how to use this pace in order to break through the opposition defensive block.

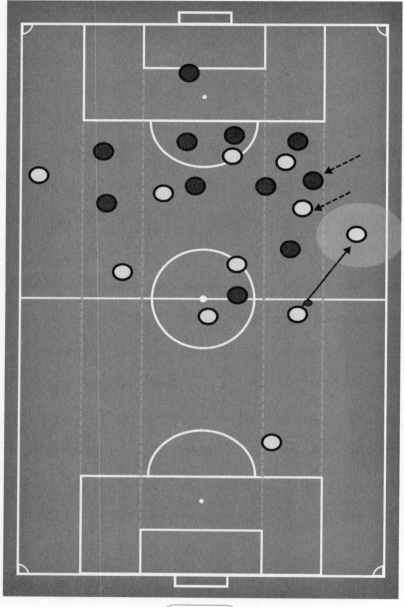

Figure 48

There are, of course, some times when City are in possession that the actions of Kyle Walker at right-back have to be more understated. These are most often when City are still in the process of securing possession, with their own players moving into the positions they are expected to occupy in the attacking phase. In circumstances like this, Walker will not look to immediately move to a high line in the wide area but will create angles that offer support to the man in possession.

We can see this in *figure 48*. With the right-sided central defender in possession of the ball, we see the player on the right of the forward line make a small diagonal movement out of the wide zone and into the half-space. This movement empties the space in the wide area into which Walker is free to move. Instead of immediately moving to a high line when space is created we see him retain a slightly deeper position to make the pass from the defender much more simple.

This lack of movement from Walker is very simple but it is key in allowing the attacking phase for City to develop properly. As he takes possession, City have created a slightly advanced platform from which they can play. Moving the ball from the first line, with the central defender, to the second line, with Walker, makes the next pass into the final third much easier. As Walker takes the ball in this area there will be three passing options that develop for him, and the wide forward will retain his position in the half-space in a supporting position. Ahead of the ball, however, the '8' who is advanced in the half-space will move across to occupy the wide area; this movement takes a defensive player out of position and opens up the half-space. This, in turn, creates the opportunity for the forward player to make an angled run through the half-space. Walker then has three options to progress the ball: inside, forward to the wide area, or through into the penalty area with the run of the forward player. Once again it is important that Walker understands the tactical requirements of the role that he plays as well as those of the wider tactical structure around him.

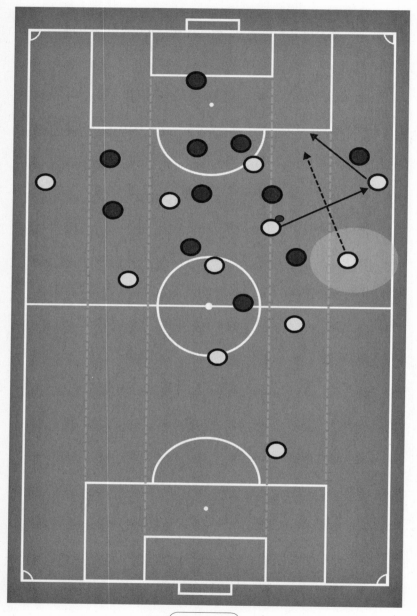

Figure 49

The main piece of information that Kyle Walker has to be able to process when deciding on his positioning or on his runs is the positioning of the wide forward ahead of him. The choice is relatively simple: if the wide forward is in the wide area then Walker moves to the half-space. If the wide forward moves into the half-space then Walker occupies the wide area. Of course, the picture is further complicated when you take into account the positioning of the '8' on the right side of the field. Once again the identity of the player who fill this role may dictate the position that Walker will occupy in the attack. Kevin De Bruyne, for example, is more likely to stay in central areas and leave the half-space for Walker to occupy while Bernardo Silva will drift into the half-space. The importance of understanding the tactical picture ahead of him and identifying the spaces that he needs to occupy are key in the role that Walker plays for City.

In *figure 49* we see a situation where Walker is able to advance forward on a diagonal line to occupy the half-space on his side of the pitch. Once again the key piece of information for him to process comes in the connecting pass between the '8' and the wide forward. As that pass is made, Walker makes a diagonal run to a high line in the half-space. This run, in turn, allows the wide forward to play the ball through into the path of Walker as he advances forward and threatens the penalty area.

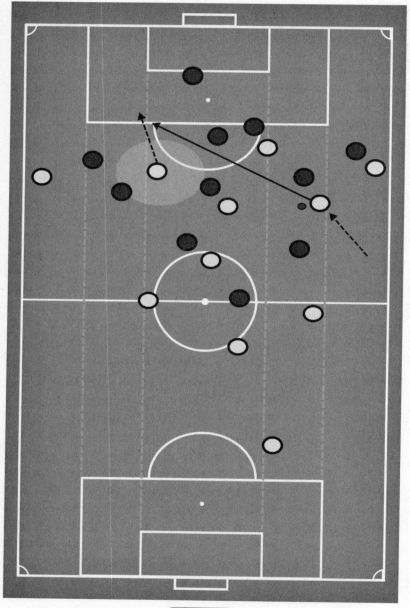

Figure 50

What is perhaps most impressive when it comes to the role that Walker plays within this City side is the development of his understanding of passing lanes and angles over the last two seasons. In the early stages of his career, he was a more straightforward player who would pick up the ball either deep or in advanced areas and look to do one of two things: either drive at the nearest defender to try to dominate them in a 1v1 situation, or he would cross the ball into the penalty area. There was no grey area in this thinking and no thought of engaging in intricate build-up around the edge of the penalty area.

Over the last two seasons under Pep Guardiola, we have seen a huge shift in the way that Walker sees and understands the game to the point where we now have situations like that displayed in *figure 50*.

In this example we again see Walker using the half-space as he moves into the final third of the field. The difference in this example is that he drives into this position with the ball at his feet instead of moving inside in order to receive a pass. When he moves across in possession from the wide area to the half-space he forces a defensive player from the opposition to move out to engage with him in an effort to win the ball. It is at this point that the previous version of Walker would have run into a dead end and tried to use his pace and power to move beyond the defender. Now, though, as the defensive player moves out to engage the ball Walker has the ability and the vision to recognise that the space in the defensive structure is across in the opposite half-space. He is capable of not only seeing this pass but also completing the ball that released a team-mate through this space and into the penalty area.

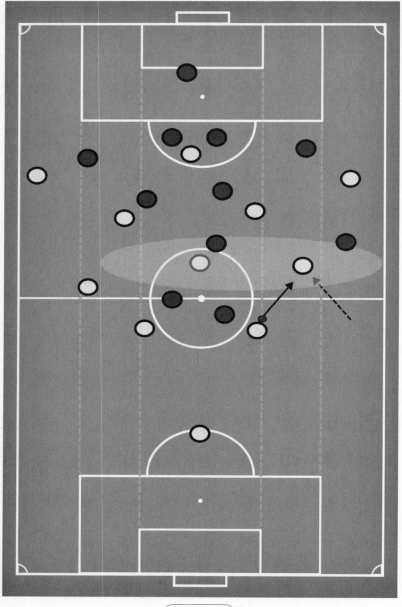

Figure 51

We have already seen the important role that the full-backs play under Guardiola when it comes to progressing the ball forwards in the attacking phase. It is important, however, for us to examine the specific role that Kyle Walker plays in these areas.

One of the most important aspects of the way that he plays the right-back role is his sheer versatility when City are in possession of the ball. We have already seen above that he is capable of processing information which leads to him playing either in the wide area or in the half-space. There are other times when City are progressing the ball from the back in which Walker finds himself retaining a deep position on the same line as the '6'.

We see an example of this in *figure 51*. With the ball on the right side of the City defensive line there is no obvious reason for Walker to move; he is the next man in the chain and could conceivably receive the pass comfortably. Before taking the pass though, he has assessed the defensive shape of the opposition; there is a single and isolated defensive player ahead of him but no defensive player in the half-space. A simple diagonal run opens the space for Walker and he is able to take possession of the ball in a slightly higher position on the same line as the '6'. Remember, the first priority for City is to play the ball forwards into advanced platforms. This small positional change from Walker enabled that.

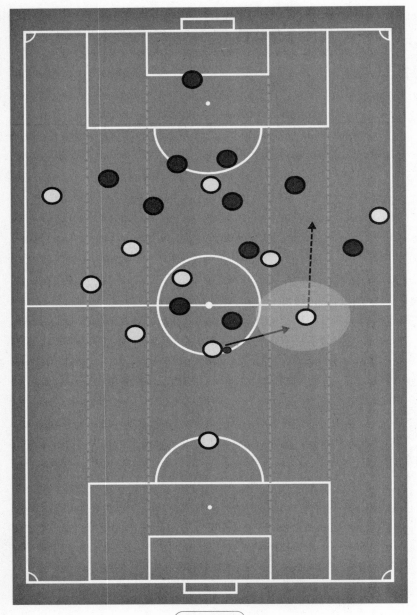

Figure 52

The final piece of play that we often see from Kyle Walker is him sitting back on the first line, along with his two central defenders, to form a back three in possession. As we now know, this is a relatively simple mechanism that allows City to progress the ball forward by shifting possession along the line until space opens in the opposition defensive structure. This space then allows the ball to be played forward into advanced areas where City are more dangerous.

When Walker initially joined City there were few in football who would have surmised that the international right-back would spend time playing as an auxiliary centre-back. Not only did Walker learn the role and the responsibilities that were expected of him in these areas, he went on to play for England in the 2018 World Cup in 2018 as a right-sided central defender in a back three.

In *figure 52* we see a situation where Walker receives possession of the ball on the right of the defensive chain. As Walker takes possession in these areas he will, of course, look to play the forward pass through the lines, always the priority! Walker also has the capacity to carry the ball forward into these gaps.

We have discussed previously that these runs can be exceptionally effective in breaking down stubborn defensive blocks. By stepping forward in this manner Walker will force an opposition player to move to engage the ball. This, in turn, will see space elsewhere in the defensive block that City will be able to take advantage of.

It is indicative of the impact that Walker has had at Manchester City under Pep Guardiola that the right-back is now an integral part of the first-team squad. His ability to work seamlessly with more advanced players in the attacking phase and form a solid defensive block in the defensive phase is extremely impressive. While the full-back position has undergone a period of undeniable change over the last decade or two, we are seeing a player who represents the next evolution of that role. The tactical flexibility that Walker displays is a key component in this City squad and he gives his coach a movable piece that can be used to create favourable overloads across the right-hand side of the pitch.

Chapter 9

John Stones

Perhaps the most important concept in the game model used by Pep Guardiola throughout his career, with Barcelona, Bayern Munich and now with Manchester City, is perhaps the methods used to ensure the clean progression of the ball from the defensive third forward.

In order to achieve this, Guardiola needs central defenders, full-backs and a controlling midfielder or '6' comfortable and confident when receiving the ball and passing it on. Gone are the days when a central defender was a purely destructive player who would be responsible only for breaking up opposition attacks. Now, central defenders are expected to be creative and have the technical ability required to play with the ball at their feet. There are few central defenders in top-level football who encapsulate this new breed of central defenders better than John Stones.

The English international defender made his debut for his hometown team, Barnsley, at just 17, having come through the club's youth system. It was a measure of his ability and maturity that the teenager did not look at all out of place in the centre of the Barnsley defence against seasoned professionals. It did not take long for people to realise that the Yorkshire club had a special talent on their hands and as tends to be the case, bigger clubs around England began to make enquiries into the availability and price of the player. This interest resulted in Stones moving to Everton, a team firmly embedded in the Premier League, for a reported £3m fee, a bargain in hindsight.

Even at his young age, Stones quickly made an impact on the first team at Everton and impressed the fans and coaches of the club with his ability on the ball and defensive positioning. Indeed, such was the impression that Stones made during his time at Goodison Park he made his international debut for England as a 20-year-old. Once again the transition to a higher level of competition held no fear for the young defender.

The arrival of Guardiola at Manchester City prior to the 2016/17 season coincided with the decision of the club to spend a reported £50m on signing Stones, a significant profit for the Merseyside club and a boost for Barnsley who had the foresight to include a clause in the sale to Everton that gave them a percentage of any future transfer, believed to be worth £7m. That City were interested in Stones should come as no surprise: the agreement with Guardiola came long before he actually arrived; as the coach was enjoying a year's sabbatical from football in New York, he would have had an input in any future deals. He was acutely aware that he would need ball-playing defenders to make his tactical system work, and Stones would fit the bill perfectly. More importantly, there were a few bad habits when in possession that would have to be coached out of the youngster's game by the new City coaching staff.

Stones went on to impress sufficiently in his first few weeks at his new club to find himself in the starting line-up for the first competitive match of the Guardiola era.

There were, however, teething issues as the young defender tried to adapt to the very specific demands under the game model of Guardiola. Mistakes were made in possession of the ball that resulted in the opposition either creating chances or taking chances. Throughout his initial period in charge of City, we saw Guardiola consistently take responsibility for these mistakes himself, making it clear that these issues were a result of the complex instructions that Stones was being given. This public approach to dealing with the criticism from fans and media alike from Guardiola was an excellent example of man management as he consistently stressed to Stones that he was a trusted part of his team and made it clear that the mistakes being made were part of the developmental process. Gradually, these mistakes abated and City began progressing the ball cleanly from the back, sometimes under extreme pressure, with Stones looking as though he was made for the role.

Indeed now, at the end of the 2018/19 season, with Manchester City having won the domestic treble, the statistical output from Stones clearly shows that he is now firmly embedded in the system. A cursory look at the defensive key performance indicators for Stones over the course of the 2018/19 season paints the picture of a player who is very much coming into his own as a first-class central defender. Over the course of the season he won an impressive 64.8% of his aerial duels, and for a player who received some criticism early in his career for a perceived lack of strength in winning aerial battles, this displays a marked improvement.

Over the course of that same season we also saw Stones make 189 interceptions, showing that the young central defender has fully assimilated into the defensive model required by Guardiola. He now reads the game well enough to stop opposition attacks before they can really become dangerous.

We also have to consider the way that Stones used the ball, given that this is the overriding strength of City under Guardiola. Over the course of the 2018/19 season he completed over 3,000 passes with a completion rate of 95%. If we drill down into that pass completion percentage further then we begin to see why Stones has been integral in the success that City have experienced over the last two seasons. He has a completion rate of 90% for forward passes and 88.5% for passes played into the final third. This shows that Stones is not a player whose statistics appear inflated through a series of sideways or backwards passes.

Over the course of the last two years we have seen Stones develop into a key piece in the first-team jigsaw for City. There were points in the 2018/19 season where he lost his place as Guardiola preferred a centre-back pairing of Aymeric Laporte and Vincent Kompany but still Stones is the defender who fully encapsulates the type of football that Guardiola wants to play.

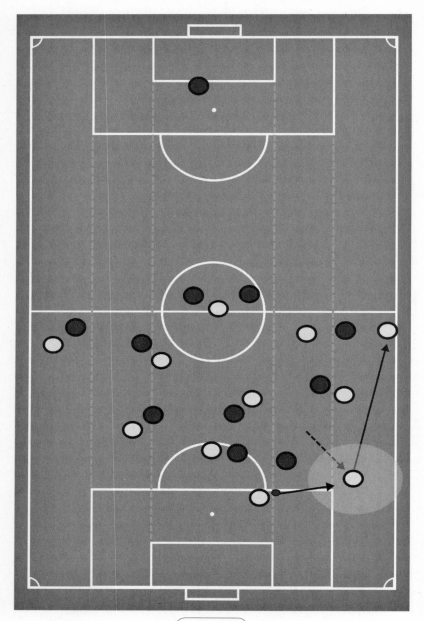

Figure 53

In the early stages of Guardiola's tenure, there were a number of clips posted on social media of City playing out from the back. They showed the ball being passed back to the goalkeeper and the central defenders sprinting back diagonally in order to give the goalkeeper a passing option, to avoid any central pressure, and to play out into the wide areas. This is still something that you will see on a regular basis from City, with John Stones being especially known for making this movement at speed.

In *figure 53* we see this type of movement being played out. With the ball with Ederson in goal the opposition are looking to apply heavy pressure in order to force the goalkeeper to make a mistake. In this situation it would not be unusual for the keeper to panic and play a longer pass to escape the press. This is not the case with Ederson, with the Brazilian having the type of ability on the ball that is normally reserved for an outfield player. As Stones makes an angled run backwards towards the corner of the field he gives Ederson the passing angle that he needs to play out of the press.

When Stones first joined City he was a capable but safe passer of the ball who rarely played from the back to the higher lines on the pitch. Now, while still being a safe and confident passer, he is now more comfortable when being asked to play to higher lines when the opportunity presents itself. This is what we see here with Stones picking up the ball from the goalkeeper and then playing out to the wide forward and away from the bulk of the opposition defensive block.

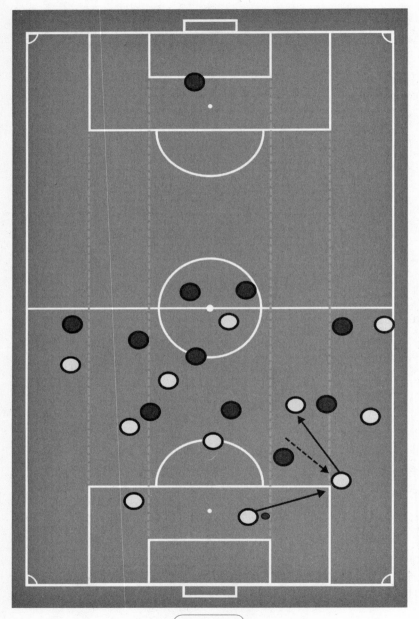

Figure 54

Figure 54 shows a similar moment from John Stones as he moves back to a wider position in order to take possession of the ball from his goalkeeper. Once more the English defender is brave in moving back to be able to receive the ball in a tight area where he could come under pressure quickly. In doing so, though, he is creating an opportunity for City to progress the ball from the back into the middle third, something that we have already seen is integral to the attacking game model favoured by Pep Guardiola.

As Stones takes possession of the ball on this occasion, he has Kyle Walker at right-back offering a diagonal option. The position of Walker, though, draws an opposition player out towards him and this of course has a knock-on effect to open up space inside that Stones can play into. This means that as the '8' on that side, Kevin De Bruyne this time, drops back into the half-space, he is able to take possession of the ball from Stones. This pass back inside also catches the opposition defensive block slightly off balance as they are shifting across towards the City right as the ball moves back in the opposite direction.

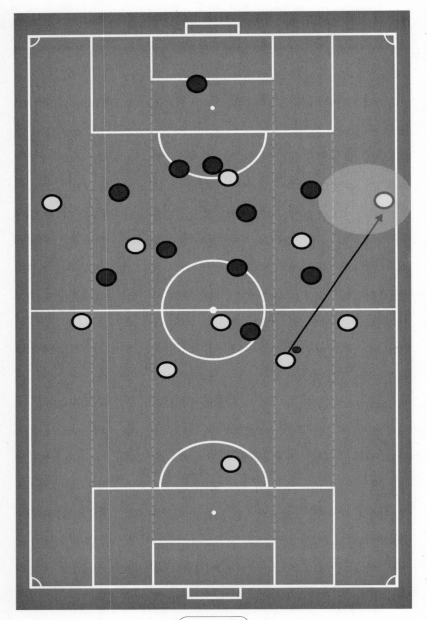

Figure 55

We have seen examples above of the manner in which John Stones will drop back in order to help his team-mates to progress the ball from the first line of the City structure. He is also exceptional at finding passing lanes and angles in order to unbalance the opposition defensive structure and press.

Figure 55 shows an example of Stones being able to access all areas of the field with his passing range. Indeed, over the course of the 2018/19 season Stones completed an impressive 69.4% of his passes over a longer distance. As he collected the ball in this example, City were firmly in the possession stage of their attacking phase as the opposition were starting to abandon the press to drop back into a more compact defensive block. The one forward player for the other side cannot get across to put enough pressure on Stones in possession and the defender is able to play the ball wide out to the right-hand side where the wide forward is in a strong position.

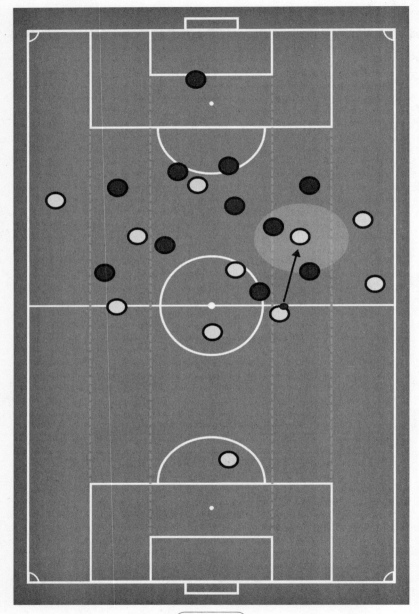

Figure 56

As well as being comfortable when passing the ball over longer distances, John Stones is also capable of more nuanced passes that split defensive blocks to find team-mates in pockets of space.

In *figure 56* we again see Stones in possession of the ball in the first instance as City look to progress from the middle third forward and into the final third. Despite there being three opposition players positioned in close proximity to the ball, Stones is still brave enough to pass the ball into pressure where Bernardo Silva, as the '8', has dropped into a pocket of space in order to receive the ball.

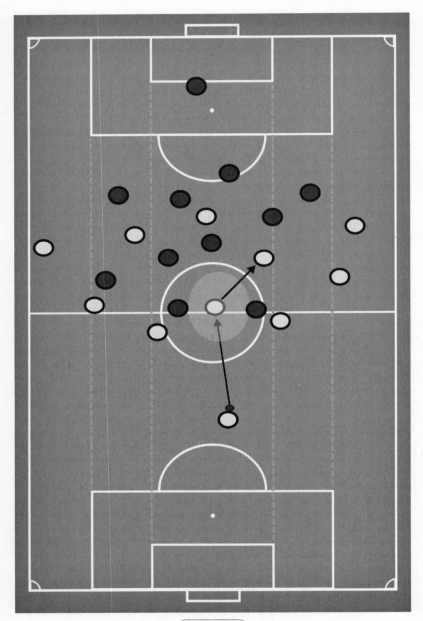

Figure 57

At times over the course of the last two seasons we have seen Pep Guardiola experiment with the use of John Stones as as the '6' at the base of the midfield when Fernandinho is not available for selection. The thinking behind this switch is fairly simple as Stones already possesses the passing ability to play in that area but he also has arguably a more advanced defensive acumen than any of the other replacements for Fernandinho in his role.

Figure 57 shows an example of Stones in this position. You will notice from the graphic that as the deepest midfielder, he sits in a deeper still position and indeed he almost splits the two central defenders on a line that is just ahead of them.

Positionally there were definite signs that Stones was not quite comfortable with the role; he preferred to remain in deeper areas where he would be able to support the central defenders as the opposition looked to launch counter-attacks. Where Fernandinho would make delayed runs into advanced areas in order to support the attack, Stones would err on the side of caution.

That is not to say that the English international will not grow more comfortable with playing in this role. We have already see that the young defender is coachable and takes instruction well. Perhaps after a full pre-season on the training field we may see Stones used in this role more often going forward.

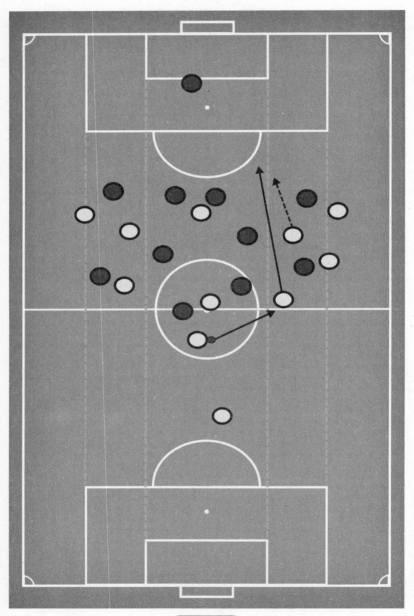

Figure 58

While Stones is somewhat uncomfortable in the '6' role, we have seen him taking up a position on the same line as the '6' when City are in periods of sustained possession. Against sides that look to sit in low, compact defensive blocks the central defender will press forward to offer a passing lane to the side that may open the ability to play forward into more advanced spaces.

Figure 58 is a case in point. As the opposing side drops back and looks to start forming a more compact defensive block, we see Stones step forward from the first line to the second line, level with the '6'. As the ball is fed into him in this area the vertical passing option is opened up and Stones is able to release Bernardo Silva, who is playing as the '8' on the right side.

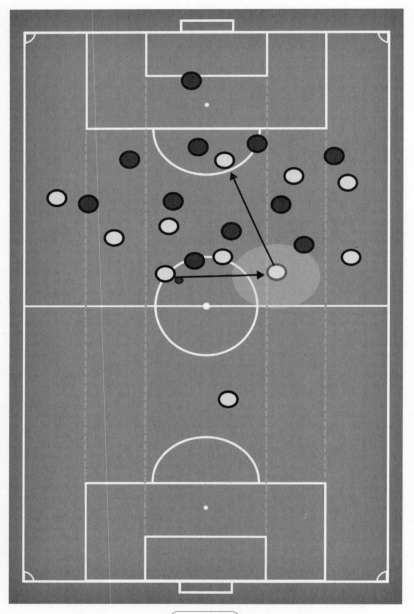

Figure 59

We see a similar story in *figure 59* where this time the entire first line for City has stepped well into the opposition half. As the ball is played across and into John Stones from Aymeric Laporte, who was his central defensive partner, we see a passing lane open up.

From this area Stones plays diagonally to the furthest line where Sergio Auguero is in a position to collect possession of the ball. The forward player is then able to hold the ball up and play from an advanced platform as he brings others into play around him.

The fact that Stones is willing and able to play these types of passes, and play them accurately, is a huge plus for Pep Guardiola in implementing his game plan. Stones displays an understanding of passing lanes and angles that would compare well with a creative midfielder. What is key for the English defender is to find a way to balance the attacking demands of his position with the defensive responsibilities. As he matures as a player and continues to learn, I would expect him to make fewer defensive mistakes as he transitions towards becoming a top-class central defender.

With Vincent Kompany having announced that he is leaving City, to become player-manager at Anderlecht in his native Belgium, there will be a bigger role for Stones to play next season. This will be his time to show that he is capable of living up to his huge potential. After two full seasons of training and playing for Guardiola we should now see Stones ready to be fully assimilated into the tactical structure wanted by the Spaniard.

Chapter 10

Aymeric Laporte

We have already seen that one of the most important concepts used by Pep Guardiola comes in the way Manchester City play through the thirds of the field and, most importantly, the way his team secure clean ball progression from the defence. During the course of the 2018/19 season, the central defender Aymeric Laporte emerged as a key figure in securing possession in these areas.

The French international had been a transfer target for City prior to the start of the 2017/18 season. His club at the time, Athletic Bilbao, are, however, famous for their reluctance to sell their key players. This is understandable given the self-imposed restrictions that they operate under, where they sign only players from the Basque region. The difficulty that the club would have in replacing a player as key as Laporte was significant and as such negotiations prior to the start of the season did not progress.

The January transfer window is a notoriously difficult time for clubs to find value in the market. While the first half of the season may have highlighted weaknesses in your squad, it is extremely difficult to convince other clubs to part with any players of value; after all, they have another half of the season to play themselves and their own shortcomings to deal with. For the most part, a club's recruitment department will work with an eye on the future, planning for the next two to three transfer windows with succession plans for each section of the squad. In January the process tends to be much looser. Manchester City had already built a full profile on Laporte the previous summer and had continued to track the centre-back throughout the first half of the season. When Athletic Bilbao were faced with the prospect of losing Laporte they identified Inigo Martinez as the only Basque central defender capable of replacing him. Unfortunately, there was one small problem. Real Sociedad are fierce rivals of Athletic and although Martinez had a release clause in his contract, as is required by law in Spain, the player himself was not interested in making the move. That was what ended the chances that Manchester City had of signing Laporte in the summer.

As the first half of the season wore on, however, Laporte continued to impress and City, correctly, identified a weakness in the depth that they had in the centre of defence. This coincided with a softening of the stance of Martinez in terms of a potential move to Athletic.

These factors resulted in City being able to complete a reported £57m deal to take Laporte to Manchester with Martinez, in turn, moving to Athletic for £32m. A notable profit for the Basque side.

Over the course of his first six months in Manchester Laporte acclimatised well and quickly became an important part of the first-team squad. It was in the 2018/19 season, however, that he really emerged as a key component of the City team. Most comfortable playing in the centre of the defence but also capable of playing at left-back, the versatility of Laporte became extremely important for City following the serious injury suffered by left-back Benjamin Mendy. Some of the statistical metrics that we saw from Laporte over his first full season at the club further emphasise the impact that he has had at the club. A 92.7% pass completion ratio along with an 88.4% success rate of his passes played forward and an 88.5% success rate of passes played into the final third of the field show that in possession he was a key factor in City progressing the ball cleanly through the defensive and middle thirds of the field. Laporte also registered an impressive 58.5% success rate when it came to aerial duels as he became arguably the most important central defender at the club.

Indeed, the defensive side to Laporte's game is often overlooked as he is seen very much as a ball playing defender. While he is strong in his use of the ball and understanding of when and how to progress the ball forward in Guardiola's system, he is also often the first defender to engage the ball when the opposition look to launch a counter-attack. For a French defender raised in the Spanish game, Laporte has a lot of hallmarks of a central defender more in the traditional English mould. He enjoys the physical side of the game as much as he does the technical and tactical side.

What is especially impressive about the approach of Laporte in the defensive phase is that he is equally comfortable defending in wide areas, when isolated against an opponent, as he is in central areas. Traditionally, central defenders would find it more difficult to defend when the opposition played quickly in transition into wide areas. With the full-back out of position, the central defender would be expected to pull across to defend in the wide spaces. In today's game, with full-backs becoming far more involved in advanced areas, it is even more important that central defenders have the flexibility to defend across the full width of the field. This is again where the tactical flexibility of Laporte comes into play. Given that he is comfortable when used traditionally as a central defender but also when used as an auxiliary left-back, it stands to reason that he would be equally comfortable defending anywhere on the field.

With the likes of Nicolas Otamendi and Vincent Kompany approaching the latter stages of their career, and with injury being a concern for both, the signing of Laporte proved an astute piece of business for City, despite the relatively high fee.

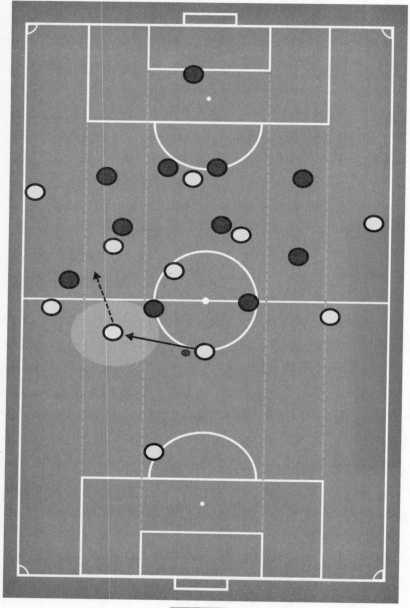

Figure 60

The first aspect of Aymeric Laporte's game that we will look at more closely is his ability to break the opposition lines in possession of the ball. We have already seen that this is an important aspect of the way that City look to progress the ball forward. The overriding priority when playing out from the back is for City defenders to have the capacity and the confidence to find passing lanes through the opposition that allow them to create more advanced platforms to play from.

We have already discussed this concept in detail in our opening chapter as well as touching on the capacity of the likes of Kyle Walker and John Stones to do this from their own specific zones of the pitch. That Laporte is also comfortable in these areas when he needs to progress the ball forward points to the fact that City value this ability in their defensive players. There is no doubt that this is an element of the game that is worked upon in some detail on the training field. This has resulted in the likes of Stones and Walker both picking up the necessary concepts quickly. Laporte, on the other hand, arrived at the club as a near perfect fit for the City system.

Figure 60 shows a situation with Laporte in possession of the ball on the left side of the defensive line. The opportunity to continue passing across to the left side where Fabian Delph is positioned as the left-back is covered by the close proximity of a defensive player. This defensive player, however, has moved across and weakened the link between him and the rest of the defensive block. There is, therefore, an open channel which Laporte can step into with the ball at his feet. Capable of playing the pass forward or driving through the line in possession of the ball, Laporte is another key piece for Guardiola in progressing the ball into central areas.

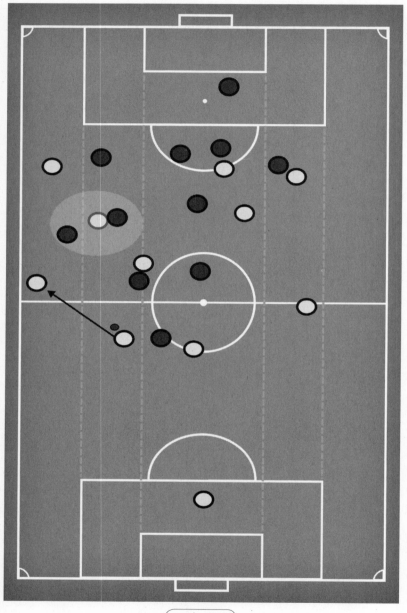

Figure 61

The onus on the central defenders when in possession of the ball is to look for the forward pass. What is important though is that these players recognise when the ball can be played into forward areas and when the ball needs to continue to circulate to the sides.

Figure 61 shows a situation when this is the case. Aymeric Laporte has possession of the ball and the opposition are positioned in order to cut off the pass back to the right side and the pass forward into the advanced areas of the half-space. The only pass still open for Laporte is across to the left side where the left-back is free.

There are some players who would try to force the pass into the feet of the '8' in the advanced lane. There are times that this pass could work if the City player can control and pass the ball again while they are under pressure but even then, the pass has a low chance of success and would not meet with Guardiola's preferred method of moving the ball.

When the ball moves out to the left-back position we may well see that the entire picture will change. The defensive structure from the other team will shift as they move over to engage the ball. The ball can then be set back once again to Laporte and this time the Frenchman may well find that the passing lane forward in the half-space has been opened up and that the pass forward can now be played.

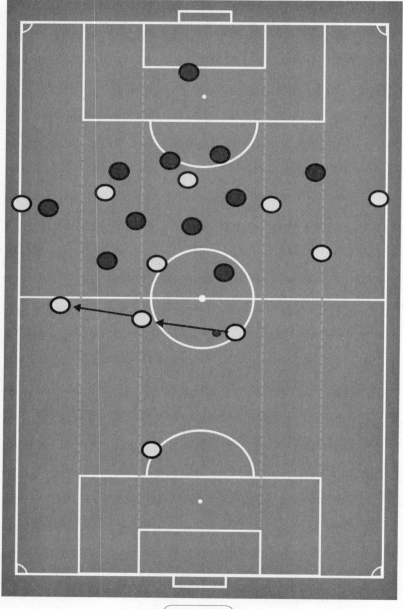

Figure 62

I do not think there is any doubt that Aymeric Laporte was signed from Athletic Bilbao purely as a central defender. The fact that he has been asked to fill in at left-back as often as he has been is a result of injuries to the likes of Benjamin Mendy and the relative lack of experience in the position of Fabian Delph and Oleksandr Zinchenko. There are points when Pep Guardiola obviously believes that the game in front of him calls for a more solid defensive option in the position and as such Laporte slots in at left-back.

For the most part, the expectations of the role remain the same. He needs to progress the ball and work in the attacking phase while also retaining a role in the defensive phase as part of a solid block that prevents easy access into the City penalty area. As we have already discussed, however, the way that players interpret the roles that Guardiola looks to use depends on their own individual identities. We are less likely to see Laporte looking to move high in the attacking phase or make overlapping runs towards the penalty area. Instead, he will adopt more cautious positions and angles to offer support to the player in possession of the ball ahead of him.

Figure 62 shows this. As City have possession with their central defenders, we see that on the right side Kyle Walker has advanced higher, into the half-space, while Laporte retains a deeper position. He is then able to collect possession wide on the left before looking to play forwards.

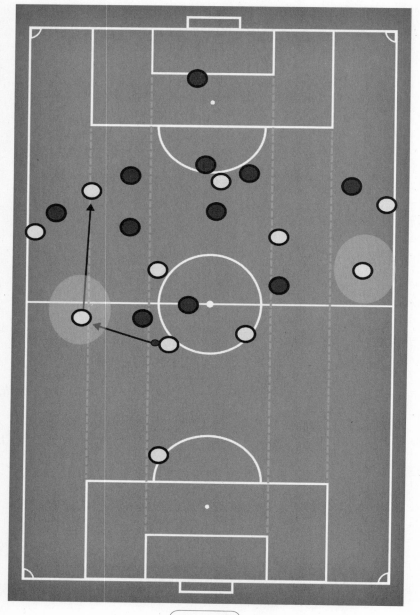

Figure 63

We see a similar situation in *figure 63* with the ball coming across the defensive line once again. The difference in the positioning of the full-backs is once again notable, with Kyle Walker having moved to a higher line on the right-hand side already. Aymeric Laporte, at left-back again, retains a deeper line and the ball is fed across to him in space.

Again we see the priority in possession coming into play as Laporte makes the vertical pass to the player in the half-space and City are straight away working from an advanced platform from where they can threaten the opposition penalty area.

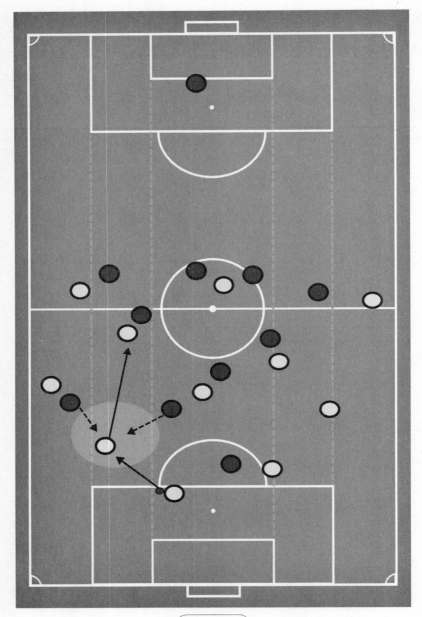

Figure 64

There are few, if any, central defenders in European football who are as comfortable on the ball as Aymeric Laporte. The French defender is capable of receiving the ball in tight areas and playing through pressure from the opposition. The term press-resistant refers to a player's ability to take possession under pressure and stay on the ball to make a positive action, whether that is a dribble, a pass or a shot. The term is usually reserved though for players that operate in more advanced areas but it can also be applied to Laporte given the calm manner that he shows when under pressure.

Figure 64 shows this. As Laporte takes possession of the ball from Ederson he is immediately under pressure as two opposition players press in towards the ball to try to prevent Laporte from playing forwards. Instead, though, we see him stay on the ball before finding the pass to a player in a more advanced position.

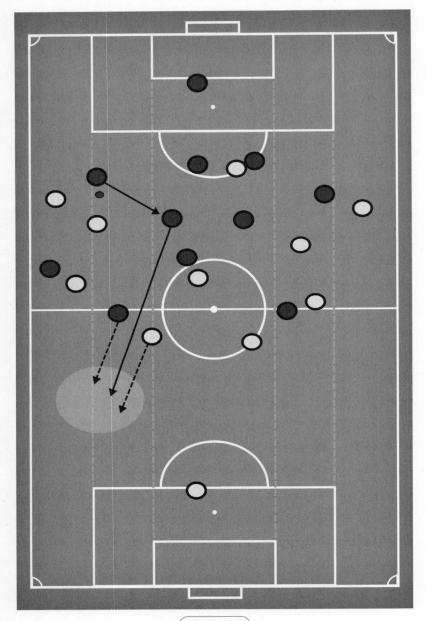

Figure 65

Laporte has to be able to play intelligent passes and take positions that support the man in possession but we have to remember that the primary role of the central defender has to be to prevent the opposition from breaking through and creating goalscoring opportunities.

Under Pep Guardiola we see Manchester City push their defensive line high in order to support the attacking phase. Despite the tendency of City to counter-press (as we have already seen) when transitioning from attack to defence, there is still a risk that the opposition will play a direct pass over the top of City's defence.

Figure 65 shows one such example. As the ball is played by the other team over the top of the City defence, Laporte has to react in order to collapse back and close down the space that has been left behind. As the ball is played over the top he has the pace to close the space and reach the ball first – and as we have already discussed, he is comfortable enough defending when isolated in wide areas to deal with the threat.

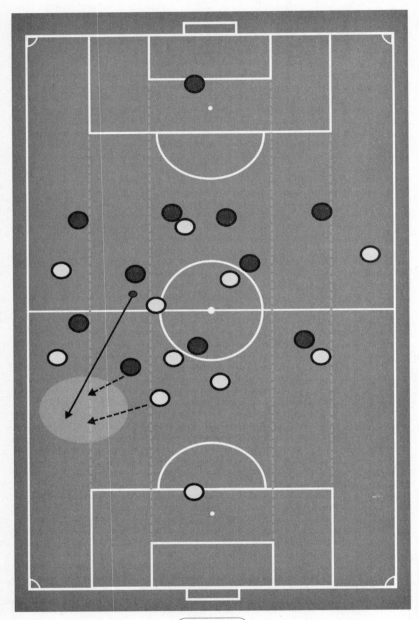

Figure 66

We see the same situation in *figure 66* with the opposition trying to play quickly in the transition from back to front. Once again with the left-back for City caught on a higher line at the moment when they lose possession, the opposition target this zone to try to get in behind the City defensive line.

Again though, the pace and anticipation of Aymeric Laporte is enough for him to recover backwards quickly enough in order to win the ball and regain possession for his side. This pace is key for Pep Guardiola in being able to push his defensive line into more advanced areas without being afraid of the potential for the opposition to hit quickly in transition with direct passes.

The signing of Laporte felt like a watershed moment in the history of Manchester City over the last two seasons. Signing him gave Guardiola a defensive piece that could fill a variety of different roles in the defensive structure, whether at left-back or in the centre of the defence. It is a measure of the importance of Laporte that he very quickly became a key part of the first team. A fantastic passer of the ball and a player who not only understands but also excels in the defensive phase, he is the all-around defensive player who makes the game model of Guardiola work.

Chapter 11

David Silva

Make no mistake about it, Manchester City are a club with a long and storied tradition. Fans of the club are intent on pointing out to people that the club existed long before the 2008 takeover that saw them elevated to become one of the richest clubs in football. During their more recent history, City had even spent time in the third tier of English football as they appeared to suffer one mishap after another. Whereas normally I would be keen to give even more detail on the historical significance of the club, we have to accept that this book is concentrating on just the last two seasons.

Since the 2008 takeover by the Abu Dhabi United Group, there is perhaps no single player that better represents Manchester City than David Silva. Originally a product of the Valencia youth system, he stood out in a team that also contained David Villa, Jordi Alba and Juan Mata.

So often he was the creative spark that created chances for Villa to convert and Valencia were one of the most exciting young sides in Europe. In 2010 Silva agreed to leave Valencia to join the project at City for a reported £25m, a bargain of monumental scale in hindsight. Indeed, in order to complete the same transfer today, it is likely that City would likely have to spend at least three times that figure.

The value that City have extracted from that deal is staggering. Yes, Silva is very well compensated in terms of his wage and that outlay over the eight-year period is, when combined with the transfer fee, a large one. What Silva has provided in return, though, has been more than worth the money. Not just in terms of goals, assists or key passes. Often, Silva has represented the heartbeat of this team, tying the game together on the pitch and proving an inspirational figure off it. The way that Silva is seen by the squad as a whole was shown when, in 2017, his son was born prematurely. Pep Guardiola, quite rightly, allowed Silva to choose when he would and would not play or train and encouraged the midfielder to spend as much time with his family as possible. Thankfully, the younger Silva made a full recovery but during that period the entire City side rallied around Silva and winning each match in support of Silva and his son became a key focus of the City squad as a whole.

The role played by Silva during his time at City shifted as he operated under a succession of coaches. Under Roberto Mancini and Manuel Pellegrini, we saw him used very much either as a traditional number '10' or as a playmaker in the wide positions. When Guardiola took charge of the club, though, we saw a definite shift in expectations on Silva. In the 4-3-3 structure, he has been used almost exclusively as one of the two number '8's in the centre of the midfield.

We have already seen the importance of this role as City operate almost with hybrid '8's/'10's under Guardiola, with the expectation being that Silva, in particular, operates in a far more advanced position when the team are in possession of the ball. Indeed, when City attack we often see Silva position himself in the left half-space where he is able to receive possession between the lines of the opposition and cause havoc.

The impact of Silva has never been as simple as goals and assists. In the 2017/18 Premier League season he registered nine goals and ten assists while in 2018/19 those numbers fell to six goals and seven assists. Instead, it is about his ability to operate in tight spaces to find space in tight compact defensive structures and create paths through and into the penalty area. This is clearly shown in the percentage of successful dribbles that we have seen over the past two seasons from Silva: 80.5% and 76.2% respectively. Also, the success rate that he has had for passes into the final third and the penalty area over the same period: in 2017/18 he registered 87% successful accurate passes into the final third and 69.2% successful passes into the penalty area. In 2018/19 those metrics showed 83.8% and 71.3% respectively. The 2019/20 season will see Silva turn 34 and players like Phil Foden are snapping at his heels looking for a greater level of first-team football.

There is no doubt that from a purely physical standpoint he is regressing; Silva can no longer run for the full 90 minutes and his exposure at first-team level will have to be managed carefully. In terms of his ability on the ball and capacity to control the tempo and flow of the match though, there are still few in European football, let alone in the City squad, who can match the Spaniard.

The question still has to be asked whether or not Silva will accept a reduced role in the first team or whether he will be tempted to make one last big move, with China and the Gulf mentioned as potential destinations. It is entirely possible that given Silva's connection now with the city of Manchester and with Guardiola, he will choose to stay as they chase the elusive Champions League. While there are signs of Silva's ability to get around the pitch diminishing, there are no questions around the tactical and technical qualities of his understanding of how to occupy and manipulate space. These are the qualities that City would find it extremely difficult to replace over the course of the transfer window.

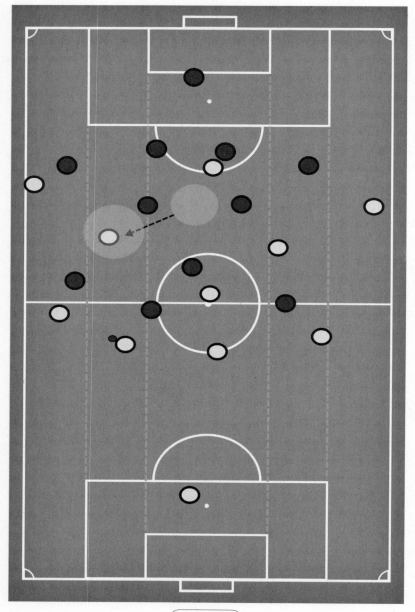

Figure 67

The most important aspect of the way that David Silva is used by City comes in his positioning. No longer just a '10', he plays as one of the two advanced central midfielders, but both tend to occupy slightly different roles. Silva spends a large part of his time in the attacking phase occupying either the half-space or the left-hand lane.

Figure 67 shows the difference between the position that David Silva used to occupy, as the '10', and the position that he now takes up. You can clearly see the difference as with the ball on the defensive line Silva would be disconnected in the central role. In the half-space, though, he is perfectly positioned to occupy a pocket of space and offer the opportunity for the ball to be played into an advanced platform. This small piece of movement is enough for Silva to create space for his side and it will also force the opposition to move in and engage him in this space. That will then cause a chain reaction with space open in another area of the other team's defensive structure that City can then look to exploit.

Silva is intelligent in his positioning and movement and will often drift between the half-space and the wide area depending on the positioning of the ball and the wide forward. If the forward player occupies the wide space then Silva will stay in the half-space; if the wide forward moves into the half-space then Silva moves wide. These movements are pre-programmed and implemented on the training ground with players throughout the thirds moving and rotating position. These rotations depend on the position of the ball, the position of the team-mates and then the position of the opposition, in that order with the ball always taking priority. Again, we see the sheer magnitude of tactical information that the Manchester City players are expected to be able to process continually during every match.

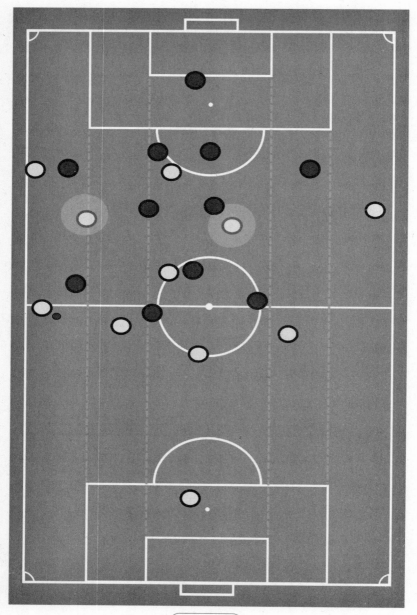

Figure 68

In *figure 68* we again see the kind of positions that David Silva would take up in the attacking phase alongside the position that the other '8' would fill. With the ball in the left-back position, the positioning of the opposition defensive block is set to deny City the space to easily play back in towards the central areas. Silva is positioned on the line that separates the left-wing area and the left-sided half-space, with the left-sided forward hard on the left wing. The other '8' in this situation is Kevin De Bruyne who is positioned centrally, and his role is to offer the pivot for the ball to be shifted from left to right as it moves forward into the final third. Silva on the other hand is positioned in order to facilitate the ball being moved forward down the left-hand side. The man in possession has two clear options but either of these will result in the same thing: Silva having possession in a pocket of space. The ball can be played directly into Silva from where he can play from the advanced platform that he has created. Alternatively, the ball can be played beyond Silva into the left forward who will then set the ball straight back to him before looking to make an immediate angled run anticipating the through pass from the Spaniard.

The point in playing forward into the final third for City is to create opportunities for the pass to be played through and beyond the last defender in order for an attacking player to collect possession with a chance on goal. This is where Silva is in his element, having the capacity to find pockets of space, to receive the ball, and then to play the incisive through pass.

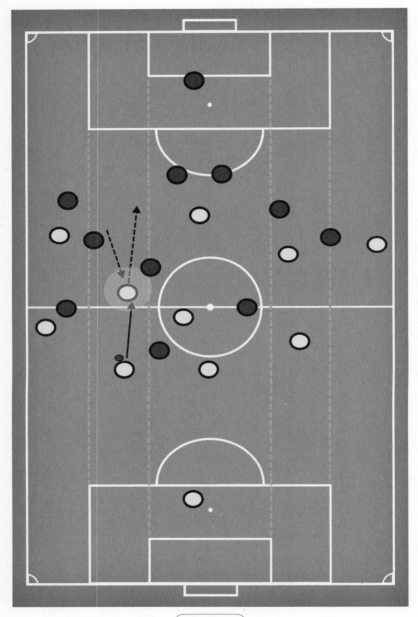

Figure 69

More so than the right-sided '8', we see David Silva looking to maintain his ability to connect with his defensive players as they are looking to progress the ball forwards. There are times, as is normal, when the City defensive players will not be able to find their vertical pass through the pressure into the spaces behind or between the defensive block. We have already seen that the ball can be rotated across the first line with each defensive player looking to play that forward pass. If the opposition are able to shift across quickly enough, though, then that opportunity can be taken away.

This is where Silva and his tactical intelligence comes into play. In *figure 69* we see one such occasion with the defensive players struggling to play forward. Silva recognises this and drops back between the defensive block in order to collect the ball in front of the block. As he takes the ball Silva has the individual quality to turn and break the lines of the opposition block, immediately placing pressure on the opposition and allowing City to progress the ball forward.

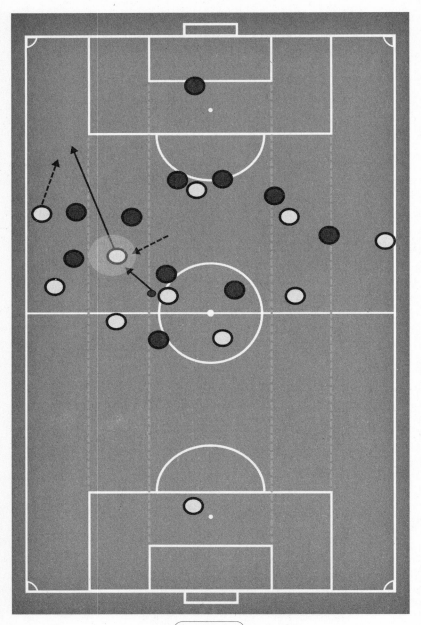

Figure 70

In *figure 70* we again see David Silva making an intelligent movement that allows the ball to be progressed past the opposition press. This time we start with Fernandinho in possession of the ball and there is an opposition player looking to apply pressure to force a mistake from the Brazilian.

The player who is pressing is also preventing the pass forward to Silva as he is blocking the passing lane. This is again where the intelligence and the freedom of movement afforded to Silva comes into play. He recognises that Fernandinho is coming under pressure and makes a short diagonal movement into the half-space. As he does so he is no longer covered by the pressing player and Fernandinho is able to escape the press comfortably. When Silva takes possession in the half-space he then has a pocket of space in which to use the ball and he does so with a pass beyond the defensive line for the wide forward to run on to.

These movements are not complicated or difficult. They are, however, extremely effective. If we run through the rules that govern the movements required of the City players then we can get a picture of the decision making at play. Firstly, Silva is positioned in relation to the ball and he is free to take possession and allow the ball to be progressed forward. Secondly, he is positioned according to his team-mates and is on the next line, ready to help progress the ball into the final third. Thirdly, he is positioned in relation to the opposition; he recognises that he is blocked by the pressing player, so a small movement still allows the ball to be progressed, still offers his team-mate a passing option, but now he is free of the opposition block.

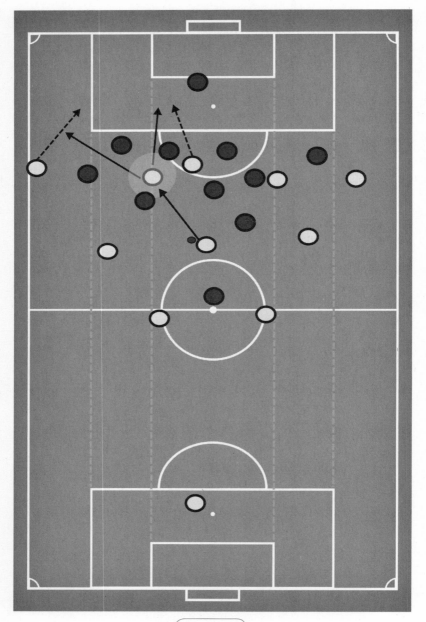

Figure 71

We also need to understand the role that David Silva plays for City in the final third and more than that, in and around the penalty area. The knowledge of space and angles that the Spaniard possesses makes him one of the key players when it comes to playing either the final ball or the pass that comes before the final ball. How often do we see City score the same goal? Everyone reading this will be aware of the goal that I am referring to. The ball is played between two defensive players for a City player running into the penalty area. They collect the ball and it is fired low and hard across the face of the goal for a player to tap into the net. The opposition will be well aware of this threat but here is the thing: it is one thing to know that this is going to happen but it is quite another to be able to prevent City from executing this movement.

The reason behind City managing this is once again simple. They execute pre-planned movements and the rotation of the ball into this area is technically executed perfectly. This all happens with Silva as the key figure in the move.

In *figure 71* we see the opposition sitting in a deep block looking to protect the penalty area. Silva, sitting on the line between the central area and the half-space, has created a little pocket of space in what is a compact block. As the ball is fed into him, this is where Silva really comes alive. As soon as he takes the ball, the advanced players of City will start to make their runs; the wide forward diagonally into the penalty area and the forward player away from his marker. They are both aware that Silva has the capacity to take possession and then play the through ball beyond the defensive line.

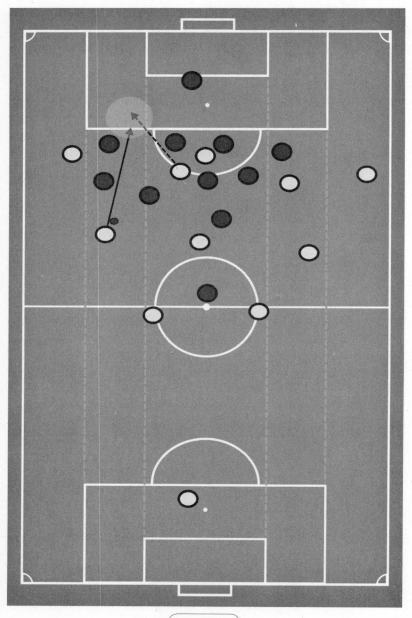

Figure 72

As well as being the key pivot for the pass to travel through in and around the penalty area, we also see David Silva operating as the player who can make the run through spaces to break through the entire defensive block into the penalty area.

In *figure 72* we see this in action. Playing at left-back Aymeric Laporte has taken a position on the same line as the '6' in the half-space. The opposition are compact and deep and Silva is positioned centrally, just off of the central striker. With the position of the ball Silva is aware of the angles and he makes a short, sharp run through the gap between two defensive players. This run allows the pass to be played and from a deep position against a compact block we see City break through for an opportunity on goal. Once again the understanding of how to use space from Silva is key in enabling this to happen.

While it is true that Silva is important for City in terms of pure leadership and character, we still cannot overlook his importance in terms of output in the attacking phase. He, perhaps more than any other player, understands and translates the game model of his coach on the field. As a player who understands when and how to position himself in order to cause maximum damage to the opposition, Silva is nearly impossible to defend against when in form. Going into next season we may see Silva lose first-team minutes, but if that is the case, the Spaniard will still be a key part of the squad both on and off the pitch.

Chapter 12

Kevin De Bruyne

Hindsight is a wonderful thing, especially in the context of top-flight football. How often have we seen players discarded by clubs, seen as not of the necessary quality, only for those players to make a return to the league with another club and suddenly unlock their full potential? Too often to count is probably the answer. Never, though, has this been seen in such spectacular fashion as with the emergence of the Belgian international midfielder Kevin De Bruyne at Manchester City.

Originally a product of the excellent youth system at Genk in his native Belgium, De Bruyne was identified as a player with potentially generational talent from a young age. The midfielder progressed through the Genk youth system and in 2010/11 he was part of the team that won the Belgian Pro League. His performances and creativity during this title-winning season, where he played either wide on the right or through the centre with equal success, caught the eye of several top sides in European football and at the end of the season, he agreed a move to Chelsea. Before becoming a part of the Blues' first team, he was sent out on loan to Werder Bremen in the Bundesliga. He handled the step-up in quality well and impressed over the course of the 2012/13 season, with the expectation that he would return to England to become a part of the Chelsea squad going forward.

At Stamford Bridge, however, De Bruyne was only exposed to first-team football sparingly. The coach at the time was a certain Jose Mourinho, who has never shown a willingness to blood and develop young players throughout his career. During that period at Chelsea, the first-team squad was largely filled with established international players with an emphasis on physicality over technique; there was, of course, no shortage of ability but players had to be able to combine the two elements of their game, and as such there was apparently no place for De Bruyne.

The Belgian is known for being outspoken and having an iron self belief. These factors combined and De Bruyne challenged Mourinho, looking for answers as to why he was not in the team and what he had to do to increase playing time. As the relationship between coach and player grew more fraught, the tension began to spill over with Mourinho reacting poorly when questioned by the media in press conferences about his young midfielder.

It should come as no surprise then that these conversations did not result in De Bruyne gaining more first-team exposure and, mindful of the need to play football in order to continue his development, we saw De Bruyne seek a move away from the club. This move came in the shape of a permanent transfer to Wolfsburg, back in the Bundesliga, for a reported £20m. It was at this point that all the pieces seemingly came together for the midfielder as he showcased the potential that others had seen for so long. Having moved in the January transfer window, he had the second half of the season to acclimatise to his new club and by the start of the 2014/15 season, it was as though a new and more complete player had emerged. He finished that season with 16 goals and a staggering 27 assists and was named as the Footballer of the Year in Germany. From being a difficult figure at Chelsea we saw De Bruyne become a team leader for a young Wolfsburg side. These performances had once again led to him being tracked by a host of top sides and Manchester City moved to complete a £68m deal, thus affording De Bruyne the chance to show Mourinho just how wrong he had been to let him go so easily.

De Bruyne was already an established first-team player at City when Pep Guardiola took over as coach in 2016 and one of the top young players in the European game. Even then, few were ready for the explosion in terms of performance and output that would come when he started to work with his new coach. Primarily used as the right-sided number '8', we have already shown in a previous chapter that under Guardiola, this role is very much a hybrid with both central midfielders operating as traditional '10's in possession. While his left-sided partner, usually David Silva, is more intent on occupying the left half-space we see De Bruyne provide a more mobile option using space on the right wing or in central areas as well as the half-space. The ability and passing range of the midfielder is perhaps second to none in world football. He is equally comfortable assisting with curved through balls from the wide space as he is driving through the centre of the pitch to combine with team-mates around the edges of the opposition penalty area. It is also fairly commonplace to see De Bruyne leading City as they transition quickly from defence to attack. He is very strong when carrying the ball quickly from the City half into the opposition half and his capacity to play the ball at speed to any section of the field makes this transition very difficult for the opposition to defend properly.

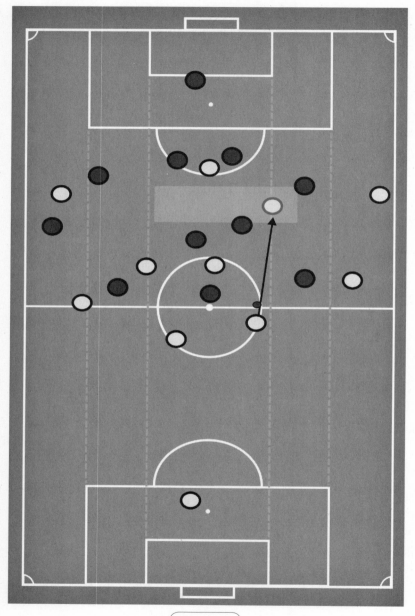

Figure 73

In the last chapter, we considered the types of movement that we see from David Silva as the left-sided central midfielder to occupy certain spaces. The picture for Kevin De Bruyne, when he is fit, is slightly different. While Silva prefers the half-spaces and the wide areas, we see De Bruyne occupy space across the central areas, the right-sided half-space and the right wing. Again we have discussed the references that Guardiola expects his players to consider when taking up positions in the attacking phase. The ball, the other City players and then the opponents are taken account of as the likes of De Bruyne drift in and out of pockets of space in and around the final third.

We see this in *figure 73* as the ball is with the right-sided central defender. On the right-hand side the wide forward is against the touchline. De Bruyne, therefore, will look to retain a position either centrally or in the half-space. The aim is to force the opposition player that is between De Bruyne and the wide forward to be caught in no-man's land. If the defender moves wide then De Bruyne has increased space to play in. If he moves narrow to cover De Bruyne then the pass into the wide area is free. A lot of the movement and positioning of the City players in the final third are designed to force the opposition to make choices in this manner.

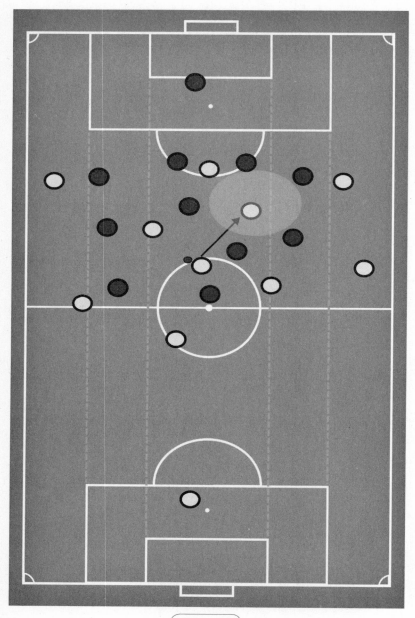

Figure 74

We see a similar case in *figure 74* as City are looking to progress the ball forward into the final third of the field. This time with the positioning of the opposition and the area that the ball is in we see Kevin De Bruyne moving across from the right half-space into the central area to pick up possession of the ball. As he takes possession he is in a pocket of space that is between five opposition players. These players will have to choose whether they press or sit back in their defensive shape.

Again we see that with this simple pass and with the positioning of De Bruyne, City are forcing the opposition out of their comfort zone. The defensive players have to make a decision and the impact of that decision can make the difference between City being able to play through into the penalty area or not.

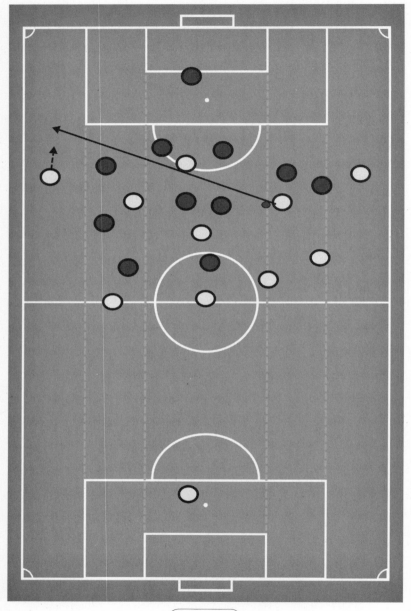

Figure 75

The problem that opposition teams have when it comes to Kevin De Bruyne is that he can kill you in a variety of ways. If you press against him then he can beat a man 1v1 or combine quickly with team-mates to play through the pressure. If you do not press and give him space then he has perhaps the most impressive range of passing in all of football. If you do not press to engage the ball then there is a strong chance that the Belgian will simply identify the space in the defensive structure and exploit it.

We see an example of this in *figure 75*. As De Bruyne takes possession of the ball in the right half-space the opposition sit off and look to deny the Belgian the space that he would need in order to play the ball through into the penalty area. Instead, De Bruyne is able to take the time to identify the space, which is on the left-hand side, and then to access this space with a driven pass across the face of the opposition defensive line.

De Bruyne specialises in this driven pass, whether across the field or through passing lanes into advanced areas. One of the overriding reasons for him having an exceptional passing range is the technique with which he strikes the ball. This is clearly seen when switching the play in this manner as not only is the length of the pass is perfect but the weight and the spin are as well.

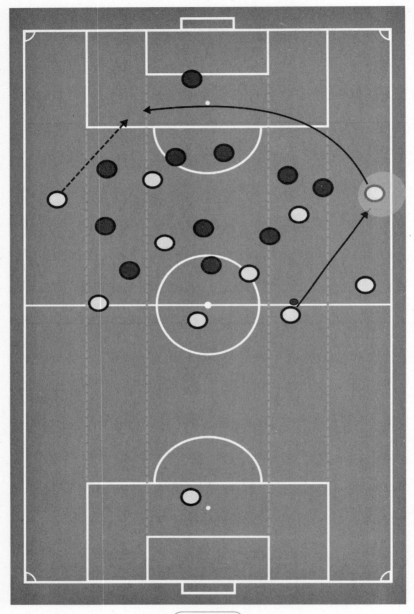

Figure 76

This passing range can also be applied when Kevin De Bruyne takes possession of the ball in the wide areas. He is superb when playing driven or whipped passes into the penalty area. The idea behind these passes is the same that we see from him in more congested central areas: to play the ball into spaces, in front of goal this time, which will allow his team-mates to move forward onto the ball for goal scoring chances.

We see this in action in *figure 76* when the ball is played out to De Bruyne in the wide space. As he takes possession there does not seem to be much in the way of direct danger for the opposition as the striker and left-sided forward are relatively deep. Such is the quality of passes that De Bruyne is capable of, he simply drives the ball with curve and spin across the space behind the defensive line. As soon as De Bruyne had taken possession, the left forward, Leroy Sane, had begun his run and he breaks the defensive line in order to collect the ball in the box for an easy goalscoring opportunity.

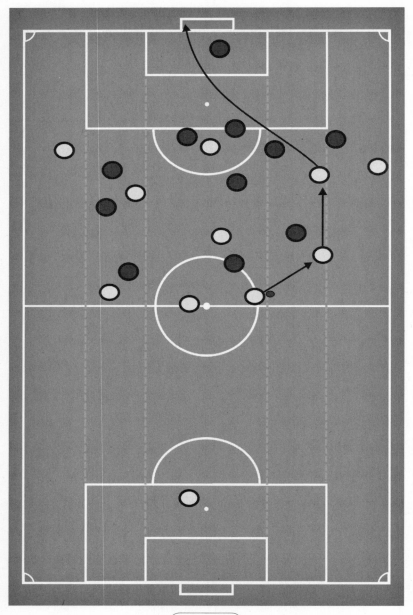

Figure 77

We have already put a large emphasis in this chapter on the way that Kevin De Bruyne strikes the ball and how this benefits City. This also stretches to encompass the danger that the midfielder carries when striking at goal from distance, especially around the edges of the penalty area.

In order for De Bruyne to be able to affect the game from these areas, however, City need the tactical structure around him so that he can collect possession in pockets of space. In *figure 77* we see an example of this in action. First, look at the position that De Bruyne is in when he collects possession, in the half-space, then look at the wide forward, hard on the outside. Finally, look at the defender, caught between the two! Once again the defensive player is not able to move in to cover the passing lane to De Bruyne because of the threat out wide. As the ball progressed through to him through John Stones and then Kyle Walker, the Belgian has the ball in space. Now, here is the true danger that De Bruyne possesses in and around the penalty area. He can combine with others or slip through balls behind the defensive line. He also is extremely accurate when shooting from these areas. In this example when he took possession of the ball he was able to strike across goal as he was in space.

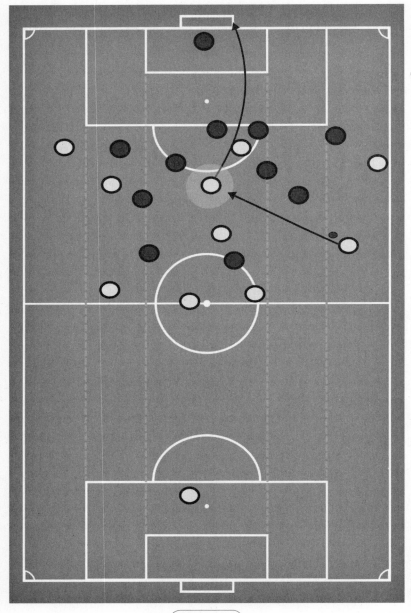

Figure 78

Figure 78 shows a similar situation, with Kevin De Bruyne this time in a central position of the field. As the ball is fed into him by Kyle Walker, from the right-back position, we see he has again drifted into a position in a pocket of space. As he receives the ball he is positioned off the main striker with no defensive player in close proximity.

Again, when he takes possession there are options open. Does he combine with Sergio Aguero, the forward player, or shoot for goal? From this area, De Bruyne chooses to shoot and scores from outside the penalty area.

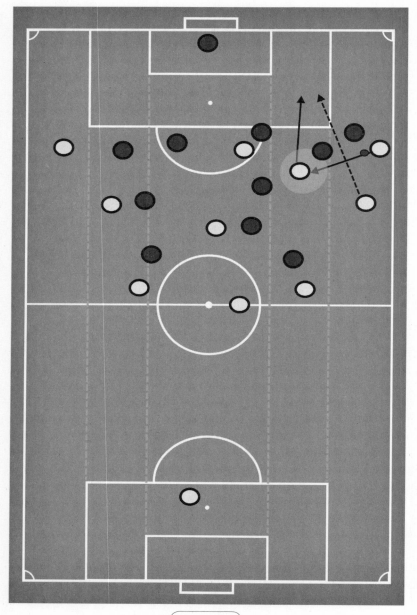

Figure 79

The final example that we will show is of Kevin De Bruyne taking possession of the ball in and around the final third before playing a quick combination to release a team-mate behind the opposition defensive line.

We have already seen in a previous chapter that the concept of overload is one which is central to the game model implemented by Pep Guardiola at Manchester City. Once more that concept is in play in this example. Bernardo Silva, on the right wing, and Kyle Walker, in a deeper area in the wide space, are going to combine with De Bruyne to overload the two defenders on that side of the pitch.

As the ball is moved from Bernardo inside to De Bruyne the two defensive players are static, believing that the threat is in front of them. It is at this point that Walker makes a delayed run between the two defensive players and De Bruyne slips a through ball past them in order to release Walker behind the defensive line. This quick combination takes just seconds but is extremely effective.

When we consider the Manchester City squad as a whole we often see that there are players who at least closely resemble others within the squad. You can swap the likes of Raheem Sterling for Riyad Mahrez or John Stones for Nicolas Otamendi and although the outcomes will be different, the drop in quality is not huge. This is not the case with De Bruyne; his playing profile is largely unique and this is what makes him so valuable for Guardiola. The capacity to create in the final third and his threat from range make him exceptionally difficult to defend against. The 2018/19 season saw De Bruyne lose a lot of first-team minutes due to injury. If City are to build on their treble season and challenge properly for the Champions League going forward then the Belgian international will have to stay fit to play a key role.

Chapter 13

Leroy Sane

There are some occasions when it comes to the development of young players where their success seems almost pre-ordained. Leroy Sane, a winger for Manchester City and Germany, is a case in point. His parents are Souleyman Sane, a former international footballer for Senegal, and Regina Weber, a former German Olympic gymnast. Both of Sane's other brothers have also played professional football, although not at the same level as the City wide player. With all of that said, the career that Sane has had to this point has been anything other than straightforward.

He was originally on the books of one of his father's former clubs, Wattenscheid 09, but he was quickly identified as a talent with huge potential and signed by Schalke 04, the club with the most well-established youth system in the Ruhr region of Germany. From this point on you would think that the development of Sane would be relatively linear; his talent combined with the coaching and facilities at Schalke should have seen him develop into a first-team player.

Instead, we saw the young attacker leave Schalke to join the youth set-up at Bayer Leverkusen, where he stayed for three years before making the move back to Schalke. In 2016 Sane made the move away from Germany, signing for Manchester City for a fee that could reach a reported £46.5m. Straight away we saw the young attacking player make a huge impact on the City squad where his combination of speed, balance and technical quality made him a difficult proposition for opposition defenders to stop.

There have been points in Sane's career in which he has been portrayed as a somewhat difficult character, for example when he was left out of the Germany squad for the 2018 World Cup, and the first signs of this can be seen with the young player's early career. This may also go some way to explaining why Sane began to find first-team minutes at Manchester City hard to come by during the 2018/19 season. There was a definite sense that his coach, Pep Guardiola, was unhappy with the attitude displayed by the young attacking player.

Taking these issues out of the equation there is no doubt in anyone's mind that Sane is an incredibly gifted and extremely effective player. Used almost exclusively from a left-wing position, when on top form he is an attacking whirlwind, full of incisive runs that penetrate the final third and threaten the opposition penalty area. In the 2017/18 season, we saw Sane score ten goals and register 13 assists in the Premier League alone. Those outputs dropped somewhat the following season, at least in terms of assists, when he scored ten goals but assisted just eight times.

The drop in statistical output in these instances, however, is likely to be more a result of a drop in playing time than of a regression in performance. In the 2017/18 season, Sane registered 2,615 Premier League minutes. This figure dropped to 1,984 in 2018/19, a drop of 631 minutes or just over seven matches in total.

A rudimentary examination of the outputs above show that Sane was no less of an effective attacking threat from one season to the next; the logical conclusion, therefore, is that there were other issues away from the public eye that resulted in the German international losing such a significant amount of playing time. There were times when the likes of Raheem Sterling, more comfortable on the right or in the centre, or Gabriel Jesus, a natural forward player, were preferred to Sane on the left side of the attack.

The development and improvement of Sane as a player since he made the move to England to join Manchester City is without question. Previously he would rely on his explosive pace in order to power past defenders into space beyond the defensive line. At City, under Guardiola, we have seen a noticeable improvement in his understanding and utilisation of space as well as in his ability when playing quick combination passes in restricted space in and around the penalty area. A confident and in-form Sane is extremely dangerous. He possesses a powerful and accurate shot and can strike free kicks from distance, as seen in the Champions League in 2018/19 when his free kick helped City past his former club Schalke. Quick and direct, he is a key component to the counter-attacks used by City when they launch the ball quickly from the hands of Ederson, in goal.

The situation with Sane as we reach the end of the 2018/19 season, and at the time of writing, is one that neatly encapsulates some of the issues that surround football today. The narrative for a lot of last season around Sane was a negative one: losing his place in the squad for the 2018 World Cup in Russia, where the Germans definitely missed the wide man, to the struggles that Sane faced to gain consistent game time with City. A lot of people around football now expect Sane to be sold, potentially back to Germany, and City fans would expect this sale to be followed by the signing of another as yet unknown wide player of the same level.

Let's take Sane out of the City squad and put him back at Schalke in the Bundesliga. Now apply all of the metrics that we discussed above over the last two seasons and consider the goals and assists that we have seen from him. Those outcomes would represent a player in which City, as a club and a fanbase, would be extremely interested in signing to fill a potential hole on the left wing. So, instead, City would be best served to retain Sane. This will also save time that would have to be spent on the training field installing all of the tactical information that a new left-winger would need. Sane is, after all, already fully up to speed with the expectations upon him in this system.

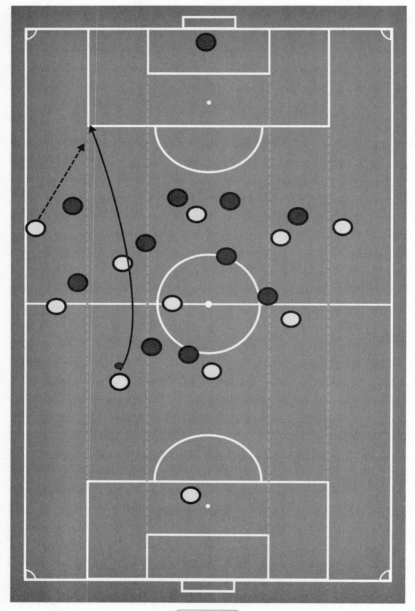

Figure 80

There is no doubt that as a wide player Leroy Sane is extremely dangerous when moving and accelerating into space. When it comes to speed over a 10- to 20-metre distance there are few players in world football who can come close to matching him. This gives City an option to play quickly in transition when they can look to release the German winger in wide areas.

In *figure 80* we see this in action as the ball is won back by City in their own half. The turnover came as the opposition themselves had played a direct ball in order to try to catch City out of position. As such the shape and structure of the opposition team is somewhat in flux. They are starting to move into an attacking structure as Aymeric Laporte collects possession and then plays the ball through the channel between the opposition right-back and central defender.

The problem that other teams have when defending against Sane in these areas is that he can wait a second before making his run. Such is his pace he can allow the defensive player a step or two as a head start before then not only catching the defensive player but also comfortably outpacing them to move in on goal.

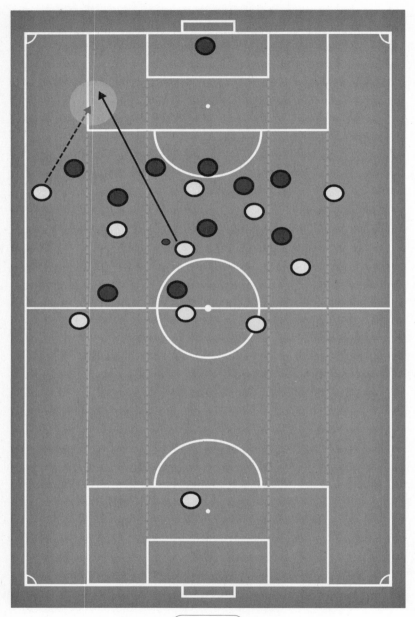

Figure 81

In *figure 81* we see a similar situation, this time with the ball in central areas, with Fernandinho, and with City in a sustained period of possession. City are positioned in their attacking structure and the opposition are set in a relatively compact block.

Look at the positioning of Sane out on the left-hand side. He is wide but he has given his direct opponent a five-yard cushion with the defensive player well positioned to the inside. Despite this positioning from the defender, the pass is still played to the inside of the defensive player and despite the positional advantage that the defensive player has, we still see Sane get to the ball first as they burst into the penalty area.

While Raheem Sterling also possesses great pace, the other options that City have in the wide area are less quick. Bernardo Silva, Gabriel Jesus and Riyad Mahrez all have other strengths but none of those possess the sheer pace of Sane. In the overall tactical structure of City, having players capable of threatening behind the defensive line in the way that Sane can ensures that the opposition does not press their defensive line high in order to constrict space in central areas. Instead, the defensive line has to play deeper and this creates more space for City players to take advantage of, especially the two '8's.

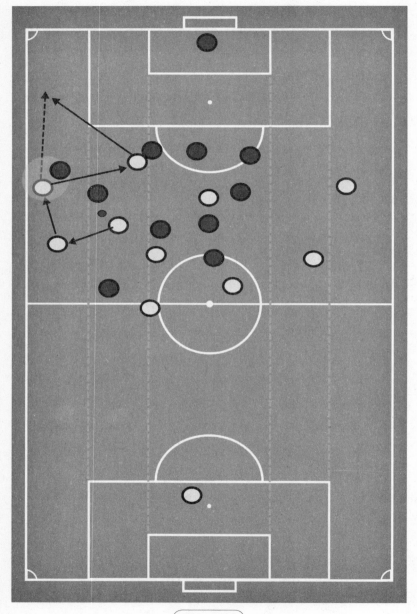

Figure 82

This pace is also used by City as they combine with shorter passes in and around the final third. We have already referenced the same goal that we see City score again and again. The one where the pass is slipped past the defensive line and we see the wide forward bursting onto the ball with an angled run that takes him into the penalty area before he then plays the ball across the face of goal. Time and time again that player making the run into the penalty area to receive the ball is Leroy Sane.

Figure 82 shows the kind of combinations that City utilise in order to release Sane's pace in behind the defensive line. The ball is circulated from David Silva, in the half-space, to Benjamin Mendy at left-back, before being played forward to Sane for the first time. The opposition right-back is too tight to Sane and a simple one-two played with Sergio Aguero creates the through ball for Sane to run on to.

This passing combination uses the overload concept in order to create impossible match-ups for the two defensive players in this area. The speed at which these combinations are executed makes it very difficult for the other team to get defensive reinforcements across to help the overloaded defensive players.

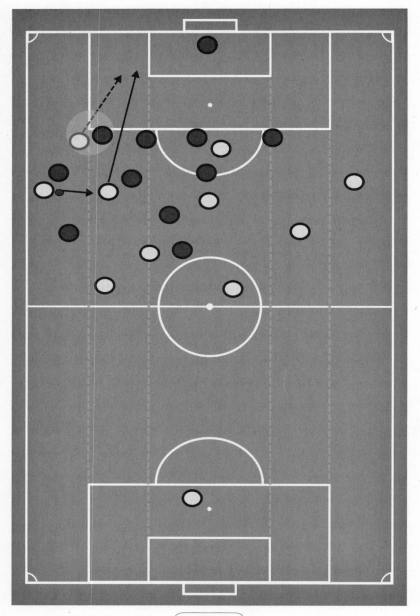

Figure 83

In *figure 83* we see a similar situation with the short passing combination ending with Leroy Sane being played through into space behind the defensive line of the opposition. This time the combination is shorter, with the ball being played from Oleksandr Zinchenko, at left-back, into David Silva in the half-space. The Spaniard is then able to play a relatively simple pass through the channel between the right-back and central defender that releases Sane to run in behind.

As with so many other concepts used by Manchester City in their game model, these combination passes are relatively simple. Why then are they so difficult to stop? A large part of the reason comes in the tempo at which City play. These combinations, around the edge of the penalty area, tend to be quick with a series of short and sharp passes that take advantage of the spaces that have been left for them. Leading up to these areas though, we often see City purposefully slow the game down with slower passing sequences before then moving the tempo back up again.

These changes of tempo are used to force the opposition out of their comfort zone and to keep them off balance with the speed increased as City reach advanced areas of the pitch.

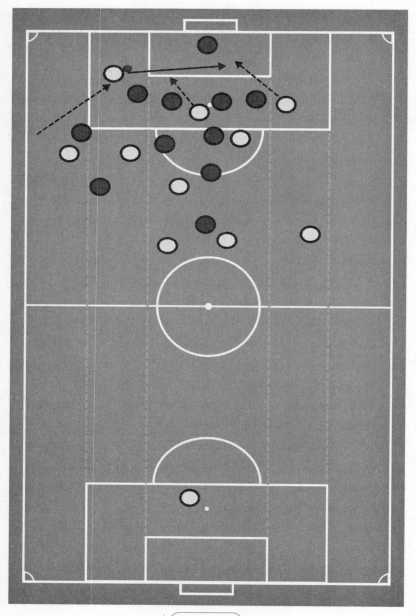

Figure 84

We have already discussed the way that Leroy Sane makes and uses space in the wide area in order to get into positions that can lead to goalscoring opportunities, either for himself or for his team-mates. It can, though, be easy to get carried away with the pace displayed by the German, but his ability to use the ball when he gets into these advanced areas should not be overlooked. Sane is a capable goalscorer who seems to favour the driven low shot across the face of the opposition goalkeeper when advancing on goal from a diagonal line. He also understands angles and passing lanes and is confident when advancing into the final third.

Figure 84 shows the kind of move that we have already discussed more than once, and once already in this chapter – as Sane is released behind the defensive line his pace and power make him almost impossible to catch. Yes, at times we will see him pull the trigger on goal himself in these areas but more often than not he will look to play in a team-mate. It is almost as though the City players take genuine pleasure in scoring goals of this type with the opposition left helpless by the execution of the passing movement. Sane is again behind the defensive line and the striker will make the near post run while the wide forward on the other flank mirrors the angle or that run to attack the far post.

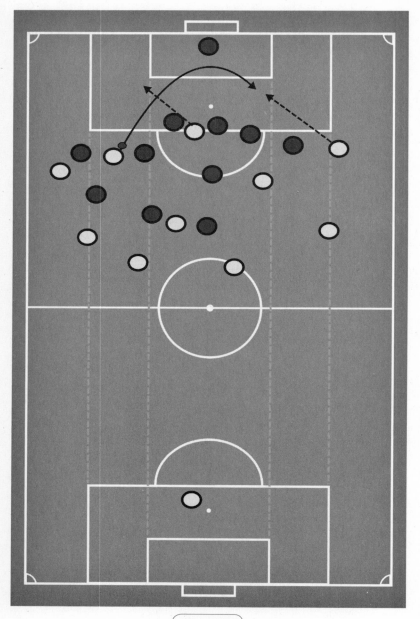

Figure 85

One of the benefits of having a player with the pace of Leroy Sane in your attacking line is the fear that it instils in your opposition. We have already discussed the fact that this pace in the wide areas forces the opposition to retain a deeper defensive line and as such opens up space centrally that City can exploit. The same principle applies when Sane has possession in the final third ahead of the defensive line.

We have already discussed in a previous chapter, when looking closely at Kevin De Bruyne, that opposition defenders struggle to know when to come tight and press and when to sit off. The same uncertainty exists when Sane has possession of the ball. Coming tight and pressing runs the risk that he will beat you 1v1 or play a quick combination and pass the defender that way. When they sit off, however, the ability of Sane to play the incisive pass is largely underrated.

In *figure 85*, for example, we see Sane in possession outside of the penalty area. As the defenders sit back and try to hold the defensive line, he is able to pick his pass and lift the ball into space behind the defensive line for Raheem Sterling to attack on the far side.

It is difficult to truly picture Sane leaving Manchester City prior to the 2019/20 season, although I am aware that this prediction could age badly if I am proven wrong. Possessing a blend of power and pace, with an incisive end ball, it would certainly appear from the outside that Sane is a perfect fit for this Manchester City attack under Pep Guardiola. The impact that he can have on the opposition, even when he does not have the ball, can be huge. This can create spaces for his team-mates across the entire width of the final third, space that can be ruthlessly exploited by this City side. This alone should be enough to make retaining the services of the German attacker one of the most important tasks for City prior to the 2019/20 season.

Chapter 14

Bernardo Silva

The argument is often made that when Pep Guardiola took over as coach of Barcelona back in 2008, he was extremely fortunate to inherit not only Lionel Messi in attack but also Xavi and Andres Iniesta in midfield. My counter-argument at these points is that at least part of the development of these players can be directly assigned to the coaching of Guardiola. To clarify, I am not saying for even a minute that without the influence of their coaches the likes of Messi or Iniesta would not have risen to their world-class status. Xavi, on the other hand, became the best midfielder in football, in part, because of the tactical system implemented by Guardiola during his tenure at Barcelona. All three players, however, became more than they were under the tutelage and coaching they received during the 2008–2012 period.

I count myself fortunate to have visited the Camp Nou in Barcelona for a Champions League match during a visit to the city in 2016. While Guardiola and Xavi were gone I was still able to watch Iniesta and Messi in person. Naturally, my eyes were constantly drawn to Messi, waiting for the Argentine to collect possession and drive at the opposition (Atletico Madrid in this instance). Unfortunately, my visit coincided with a rare drop in form for Messi. Instead, I was lucky to see Iniesta grab the game and outplay the Atletico defensive block again and again. Indeed, what struck me the most was seeing Iniesta collect possession and them seemingly drift past people in slow motion in full control of the ball. I had never seen a player display such an advanced understanding of space and how best to use that space. It genuinely felt as though Iniesta was playing the game on another level to all of the other players on the pitch.

Imagine my surprise then when watching a Champions League match the following season, on TV this time, unfortunately, when I saw a young Portuguese player who to my mind resembled Iniesta. That player was Bernardo Silva of AS Monaco. I should perhaps clarify at this point that by saying that I believe that one player resembles another does not mean that I am making a direct comparison or that I believe the two players are exactly alike. Instead, there are elements of their games which draw an indirect comparison.

In this instance, I saw Bernardo Silva take up positions in pockets of space throughout the opposition defensive block that allowed him to receive the ball and attack from advanced platforms. This was very much reminiscent of the way that Iniesta played during his peak years with Barcelona and Spain. It came as no surprise to me then when the summer transfer window opened at the end of the 2016/17 season and one of the first deals to be announced was the signing of Bernardo for a reported £43m fee by Manchester City. That season had seen Monaco reach the semi-finals of the Champions League with the likes of Kylian Mbappe, Fabinho and Thomas Lemar getting the majority of the plaudits. Quietly though Bernardo had integrated himself in the team and he became a key component to the attacking game model used by Monaco and their Portuguese coach Leonardo Jardim.

In retrospect the first season of Guardiola at Manchester City, 2016/17, ended in disappointment, finishing third in the Premier League and losing in the Champions League quarter-finals, to Bernardo Silva and Monaco. No time was wasted by the City recruitment department in identifying the catalyst of the Monaco success and realising that Bernardo would be a near perfect fit within the game model preferred by the City coach.

In some ways, the success of Bernardo over the last two seasons for City should come as no surprise. Originally a product of the extremely effective youth system at Benfica, he was identified and recruited by Monaco back in 2014, initially on a one-year loan deal. During this period there was no club in European football with a better eye for young players than Monaco. They identified potential and developed young players within their tactical system to the extent that they were able to trust a large amount of these players in the first team. This period coincided with Monaco winning the French league title, ahead of big-spending PSG, and reaching the semi-finals of the Champions League, where they lost to Juventus.

Bernardo was very much an important component of this success and at Manchester City, the young Portuguese attacker has become indispensable to Guardiola with his ability to fill a variety of positions within the tactical structure.

It is telling that whether he was asked to play as the right-sided forward or as the '8' on the right of the two central midfielders, there was no drop off in quality. Indeed the output from Bernardo over the course of the 2018/19 season speaks for itself: he ended the season with 16 goals and 14 assists over the course of all competitions. As ever, though, goals and assists tell only part of the story. Across all competitions, the he was successful with 79.7% of his dribbles. Perhaps more telling is that he was successful with 79.5% of his passes into the final third and 64.4% of passes into the penalty area. Wherever the attacker plays he acts as the focal point through which the attack is focused. He attracts the ball and connects play in and around the penalty area in a way in which few other players can. What is especially interesting is the different way in which he interprets those roles that he plays compared to his team-mates. City look a completely different side when they play with Bernardo on the right side compared to when Raheem Sterling plays on that side. There is no drop in quality but the overall look and feel of the City attack is completely different.

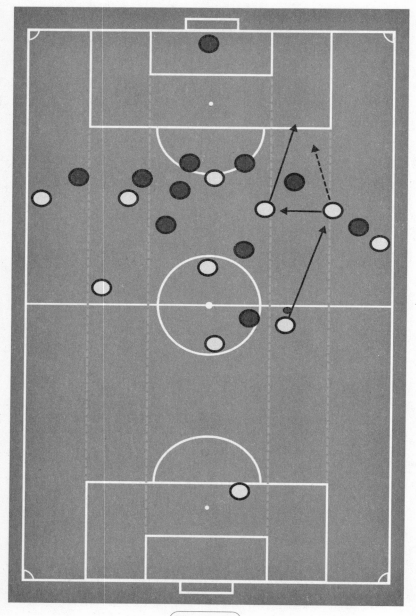

Figure 86

When Bernardo plays wide on the right he is less likely to retain the wide position and more likely to drift inside into the half-spaces. This slight positional change has an obvious impact on City when they try to utilise the overload and isolate concept that we discussed in detail in a previous chapter. Instead, on the right-hand side, we see City look to bypass the defensive block through quick combinations while the wide forward on the opposite side stays wide and stretches the defensive block out.

In *figure 86*, we see an example of this as Bernardo collects the ball in the half-space before combining with a team-mate and bursting into the penalty area. The concept is simple: when collecting the ball there is a single defensive player isolated between Silva and Ilkay Gundogan, playing as the '8' beside him. We have already seen City use these angles in order to play around or through isolated defensive players. Once again the key is in the execution and the speed with which these combinations can be played.

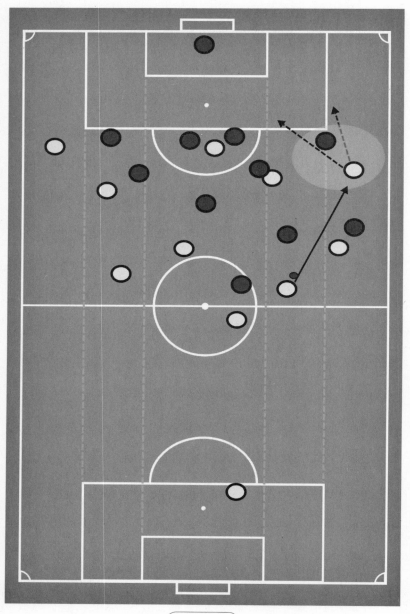

Figure 87

With Bernardo tending to shade across into the half-space when played on the right wing, he offers a sense of balance to the City attacking phase. The Portuguese attacker is a role model for young children who play football in that he is genuinely two-footed. This means that when he receives possession of the ball isolated against a single defender there is no telling for sure which way he will attack the defender.

Figure 87 shows Bernardo taking possession out in the wide area; he then has the balance and capability to attack on the inside or on the outside of the defender. This causes defensive players to freeze when faced with him bearing down on them.

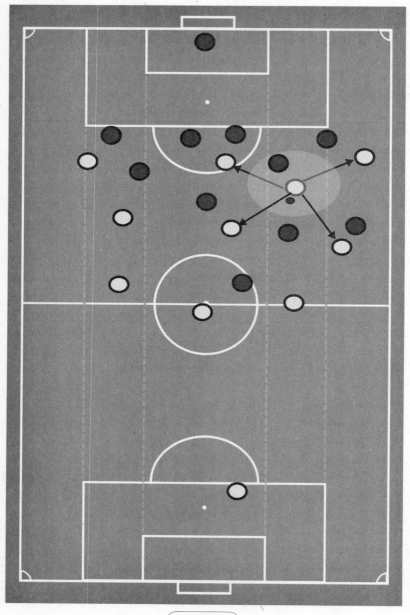

Figure 88

If the way that Bernardo interprets his role when playing out in the wide area is somewhat unique within the City squad, the same cannot quite be said when he plays inside as one of the two '8's. In these areas, he greatly resembles his namesake David Silva as he takes up positions and acts as the pivot that knits the entire attacking structure together.

Figure 88 is an example of Bernardo positioned in the half-space. In possession of the ball in a pocket of space between two opposition players we see that there are four potential passing options that he can access in order to progress the play. These passes would each provide slightly different pressure points on the opposition defensive structure.

The ability of players like Bernardo to spread the ball around in this manner is key for City when creating overloads across the width of the pitch that can help them break through the opposition defensive block.

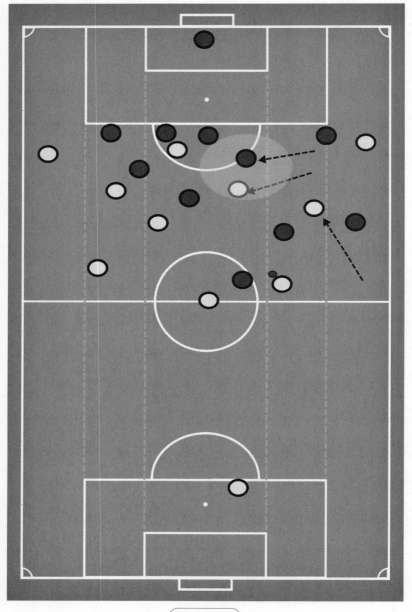

Figure 89

Sometimes a player's movement off the ball can be just as important as their movement on the ball. This is an area of the game in which Bernardo excels. He understands the need to occupy space but also the need to empty space in order to create opportunities for other players. Sometimes this can be as simple as moving from deeper positions to advanced positions, and sometimes from wide areas to the centre or vice-versa. As space is emptied by these movements it can be occupied as players shift positions.

Figure 89 gives us an example of these types of movement as Bernardo moves across from the wide spaces into the central areas. As he makes this run off the ball he drags the defensive player with him and creates space in the half-space that can be occupied by Kyle Walker moving forward from the right-back position. These movements allow the ball to be progressed forward, firstly into Bernardo and then to Walker as the Portuguese player receives the ball and then reverses it back over to the right-hand side.

Defending against this Manchester City side with the sheer number of ways that they can hurt you appears at times to be an almost impossible task. It is difficult for defensive players to retain their positions and leave the likes of Bernardo to make these runs. Instead, there will be a tendency to follow the runs and this, of course, leaves space behind that can be taken advantage of by the City players.

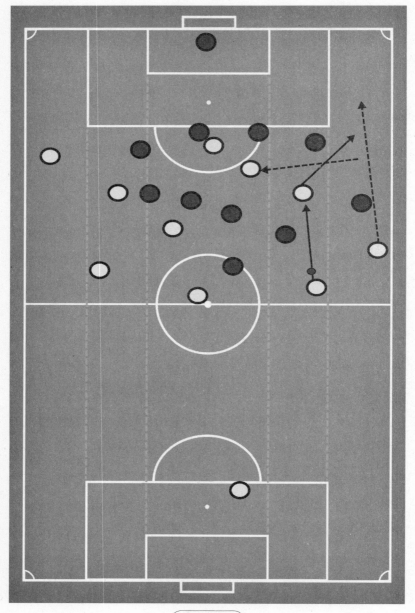

Figure 90

In *figure 90* we see a situation when Bernardo drifts across the face of the opposition from the wide area into the centre. The ball is then progressed forward first into the half-space and then out wide, while the run from Bernardo has emptied the space in the wide area. This has resulted in Kyle Walker being able to advance to a high line in the wide area, to be able to receive the pass from the player in the half-space.

These movements off the ball can often be overlooked, especially in big games, but often they can be the key factor when City are trying to break down a team that are content to sit in a deep and compact defensive block.

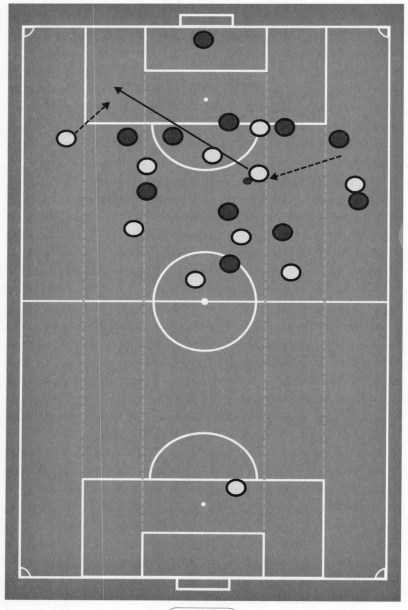

Figure 91

Bernardo is incredibly difficult to play and defend against given his vision and technical ability to complete passes while running at full speed. In *figure 91* we can see him in possession of the ball as he drives across the pitch from his original position in the wide space towards the centre of the pitch.

As he does so and while travelling at speed, Bernardo still has the vision and the capacity to identify the space in the opposition's defensive block. While travelling across, he is able to play and complete the pass through the defensive line that releases Gabriel Jesus, on the left of the attack, to move into the penalty area unopposed.

These movements are incredibly difficult for opposing teams to predict. If they step out from the defensive line to engage Bernardo as he carries the ball across, then he will use the gap that they have vacated to play the ball through the defensive line. If they manage to remain compact and deny the space for the pass through on the left then he can reverse the ball into the space that he has vacated for a team-mate by making a delayed run from a deeper position. In the end, the opposition simply cannot guard against every possibility. Once again the true beauty of the City system lies in its simplicity and in the ability of the City players to execute the simple things efficiently.

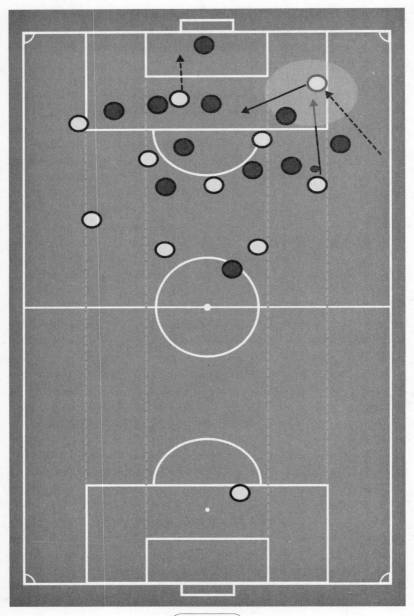

Figure 92

Our last example of the types of movements and positions that are occupied by Bernardo shows his intelligence when breaking into the opposition penalty area with space and time. *Figure 92* shows him breaking into the penalty area from out on the right-hand side. The ball is played through by Ilkay Gundogan in the '8' position and as Bernardo receives the ball in the penalty area, the expectation is that we would see the ball played across the face of goal towards the back post. He is, however, intelligent enough to know this. As the opposition collapse back towards their own goal in order to defend the cross, Bernardo instead fakes to play that way and then cuts the ball back into the space that has been vacated by the defenders moving back to their goal.

This type of game intelligence clearly shows why Bernardo has become a key player over the course of the last season for City. His understanding of the game model used by Pep Guardiola and his interpretation of his role within this model has greatly enhanced City in the time since he has joined from Monaco. His capacity to play in the wide areas or as one of the two '8's in the half-spaces offers versatility and balance to his team and enables Guardiola to use a variety of different personnel choices when preparing for matches. As a player Bernardo still has a long way to go in order to be compared fully to a legend of the game like Andres Iniesta, but there is no doubt that he is travelling along that path.

Chapter 15

Raheem Sterling

For long periods of his admittedly short career, Raheem Sterling has been something of a polarising figure. His time on the pitch has showcased undoubted potential but off the pitch, he has been portrayed, by some sections of the media, as a difficult figure. Originally on the books of Queens Park Rangers as a youngster, there was an element of controversy about the way that Liverpool secured his signature as a teenager.

Even in youth football, the talent of Sterling was well known. There were a number of larger clubs tracking his progress and it was widely expected that he would sign for one of the big London clubs. Instead, Liverpool were able to tempt Sterling north with an offer to house him and his close family on Merseyside. There were suggestions at the time that Sterling's mother was keen to see him move away from potentially disruptive influences and the move to the north west was with a view to setting Sterling on a more professional path.

At Liverpool, we saw Sterling make his first steps in first-team football alongside the likes of Luis Suarez and Philippe Coutinho. It is a mark of the ability of Sterling that he did not look out of place in a very good Reds side. Always confident when isolated in 1v1 situations against a direct opponent, the direct style of Sterling was well received by the Liverpool fanbase throughout his career at Anfield.

There were always questions surrounding his end product, with the young forward player capable of getting himself in extremely advantageous positions before often wasting the opportunities that he had made for himself. Despite this somewhat errant finishing, Sterling still operated at such a high level that he was nominated for the PFA Young Player of the Year award in the 2013/14 and 2014/15 seasons.

It was, however, during the 2014/15 season that the relationship between Sterling and Liverpool began to break down. Reports began to emerge in the national media suggesting that he was holding out to become one of the club's highest earners before agreeing to sign a new contract. It was at this point that Manchester City were able to step in, sealing a transfer for Sterling in July 2015 in a deal that could reportedly reach £49m.

In the early stages of his City career, the familiar issues that we had seen at Liverpool still plagued Sterling. His final ball was often wayward and despite finding himself in great positions centrally, he would still struggle to finish seemingly easy chances. With the appointment of Guardiola in 2016, however, we finally saw the young attacker reach his undoubted potential.

In the 2016/17 season, for example, in the Premier League, Sterling registered seven goals and six assists for City. In 2017/18 those figures improved to 18 goals and 11 assists and in 2018/19 17 goals and ten assists. This improvement in output can be directly correlated to the individual coaching that Sterling has received from Guardiola and from his role in the tactical structure at the club.

Previously, part of the issue surrounding his finishing was his willingness to shoot regardless of the angle that he had. Often, we would see him in possession wide of goal where he would attempt to shoot from acute angles. Now, having matured and received some very specific coaching on the importance of positioning when shooting, Sterling is more likely to look for the pass from acute angles.

He is also excellent at arriving in space in the centre of the penalty area when the ball is on the opposite side of the field. Time and time again this past season, Sterling has been the player in between the goalposts when the ball is cut back across goal by the likes of Leroy Sane or David Silva. Interestingly, we have also seen Guardiola over the 2018/19 season trust Sterling to take more integral roles in the attacking system. Previously, he was seen predominantly as an attacking player most comfortable when playing out on the right-hand side but he has since been used periodically in a central role either as the forward player or in the hole just behind a striker. This added versatility suggests that Guardiola views Sterling as an integral piece to his attacking system, with the ability to move across the front line in order to create advantageous match-ups against the opposition defensive players.

The greater responsibility Sterling has been enjoying for his club over the last two seasons has been mirrored by the way that he has been used by England at international level, where he has become an integral member of Gareth Southgate's squad. This greater success at both club and international level has come along with a greater maturity in the way that Sterling carries himself off the pitch. Previously, the young attacker had been surrounded by rumours of immature behaviour but during the 2018/19 season we saw Sterling speak out about racism in a manner that was intelligent and well thought out. This greater interest in social issues showed a side to Sterling that had never been seen before and suggests that the he will continue to develop in his role as a leader both on and off the pitch.

While Sterling is now a more mature figure, he still has the same explosive unpredictability that makes him so difficult to play against.

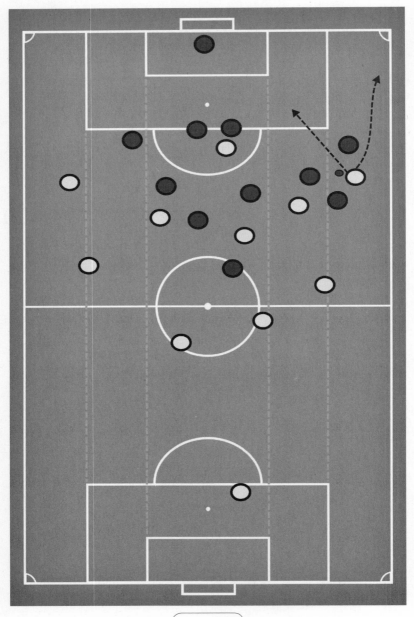

Figure 93

As we had seen previously when discussing the way that Bernardo operates when in wide areas, Sterling possesses the same unpredictable nature that makes him difficult to defend against. He has a very distinctive style when carrying the ball, with exceptional balance that allows him to change direction and attack at different angles very quickly. This ability means that we often see Sterling in possession of the ball around the edges of the penalty area as he quickly changes direction to move at speed between two defensive players. Such is his low centre of gravity, this change of direction can easily result in contact and a potential penalty or free kick if he is touched. As such, defensive players tend to back off and allow him to move into the penalty area.

In *figure 93* we can see Sterling in possession of the ball wide on the right-hand side. Previously in these positions he would almost always look to attack on the right side, on his stronger right foot. This goes some way to explain the volume of shots that Sterling used to take from poor angles that would be defended with relative ease by the opposition. Over the last two seasons we have seen Sterling develop not only the technical side of his game but also his tactical understanding of when and how to move in possession of the ball.

When he is in possession in wide areas the threat is always there that he will beat you on the outside. Now, though, he is more likely to cut back inside at pace. This movement back inside tends to result in one of two things happening. Either Sterling will be able to access the penalty area himself or play in a team-mate who can; or a second defender will be pulled across in order to help defend the threat in the wide space. As we have already seen throughout this book, when Manchester City pull defensive players out of position in this manner there will be space elsewhere in the defensive block that can be exploited.

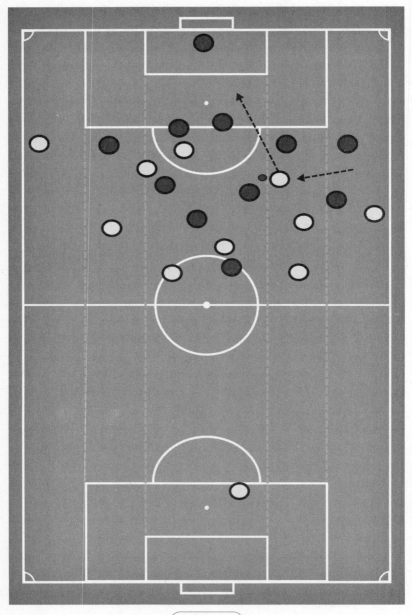

Figure 94

We see this type of movement along with the quick change of direction in *figure 94*. As Sterling cuts inside in possession of the ball he sees the gap that opens up in the defensive line and cuts through that space into the penalty area. As he moves into this area of the pitch we see him attacking at a very dangerous angle.

Once more as Sterling moves into this area of the pitch and enters the penalty area he does so at an angle that gives a much better chance of scoring should he take a shot across the goalkeeper. By attacking inside the defender Sterling has given himself a far better chance of finding the target. Had he attacked on the outside of the defender then the angle would have been tighter and the chance more difficult. At the top level of football these small details make the difference.

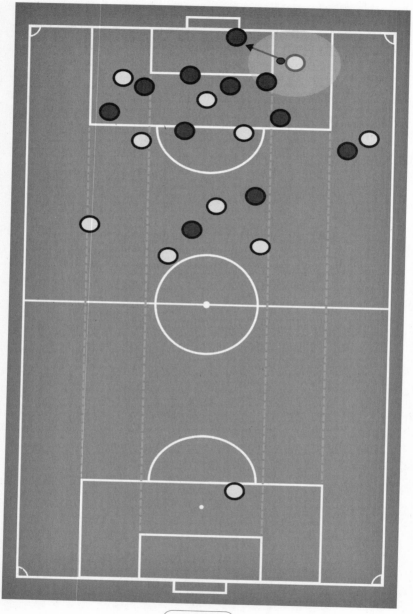

Figure 95

The differences in these angles deserve further exploration. One of the most notable trends within football in recent years has been the increase in prevalence and use of the term 'expected goals' (xG). This is an advanced statistic that attaches a numerical value to each shot at goal based on the likelihood of that shot resulting in a goal. xG takes into account a wide variety of factors including the angle of the shot and whether there are any defensive players in between the player and the goal, amongst other things. This statistic has been used in a number of different areas in football and has appeared on a regular basis as part of the famous *Match of the Day* television coverage in Britain. It has also been used to inform player and coach recruitment at two clubs run by the same man, Matthew Benham; his clubs being Brentford and FC Midtjylland.

Figure 95 shows the kind of angle and position that Raheem Sterling would often find himself in during the early stages of his career. Consider the angle and position in which the forward player finds himself: the goalkeeper is positioned at the front post and has a wide base; from this position the area of goal that the forward has to aim at is greatly reduced. There are also no other attacking players in positions that would offer support should Sterling play the ball across goal. That is not to say that he would never score from these areas. His output in the early stages of his career was impressive for a player of that age, just not as impressive as it is now.

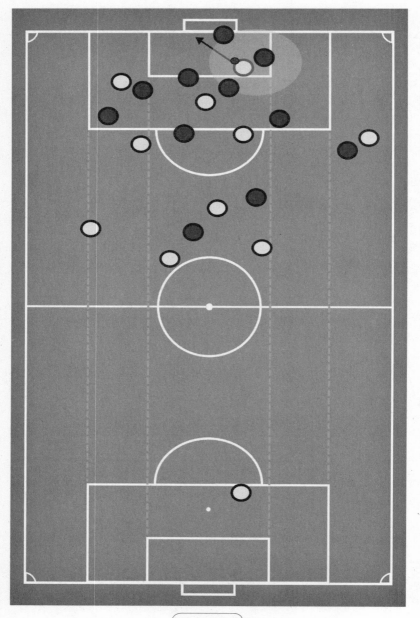

Figure 96

Now consider the position that we see Raheem Sterling take up in *figure 96*. Having initially made the movement from outside into the half-space and then into the penalty area, he is now in a far more favourable position. The xG value for a shot from this position will be significantly higher than that of a shot from the example in *figure 96*.

There is no doubt in my mind that this slight change in mentality and movement from Sterling over the last two years is a direct result of coaching that he has received from Pep Guardiola, with an emphasis on shooting from locations that offer a far greater output. The kind of movement that takes Sterling into these more advantageous positions is something that we saw time and time again when Guardiola was coaching at Barcelona. The likes of Pedro, David Villa and Thierry Henry all specialised in this diagonal movement into spaces in the penalty area from where they could have maximum impact.

The change in Sterling over the last two seasons has been dramatic. Gone is the talented but slightly wasteful young attacking player and in his place has arisen a mature and incisive finisher who is a genuine threat whenever he moves into the penalty area.

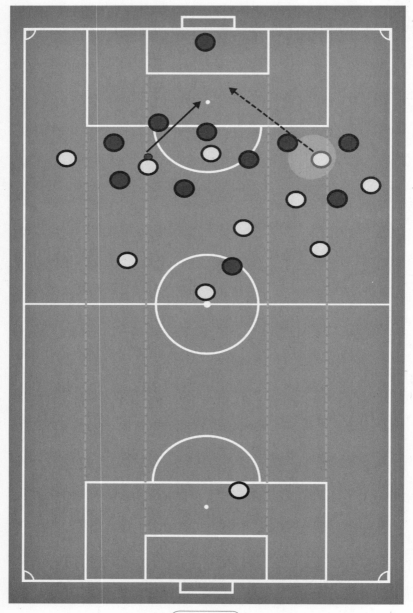

Figure 97

The threat posed by Raheem Sterling as City reach the final third is not limited to his increased ability in front of goal. He has also developed his understanding and appreciation of space and his knowledge of when to pass and when to run with the ball. Once again there is a distinct chance that the improvements in these areas made by Sterling are a result of his greater experience and maturity. He has also been a part of this City team under Pep Guardiola since the start and his understanding of the movements of his team-mates in the final third and the spaces that these movements create is excellent.

Figure 97 shows a situation where Sterling has possession of the ball in the left-sided half-space. The opposition are sitting in a compact block and there does not appear to be much space that is open that would allow him to access the penalty area. Remember, in these areas the priority for any City player is to find a way to get a clear shot at goal or to play the pass that allows a team-mate to have a clear shot at goal. In previous seasons we would have seen Sterling try to drive through the compact block, and lose the ball, or reset the ball backwards.

While there is no issue with the ball being reset in these areas, we now see the likes of Sterling, David Silva, Bernardo and Kevin De Bruyne playing passes at angles that ordinary passers of the ball simply would not see. This means that Sterling plays the pass at an angle and weight through the defensive line which allows a team-mate to play through for a chance on goal.

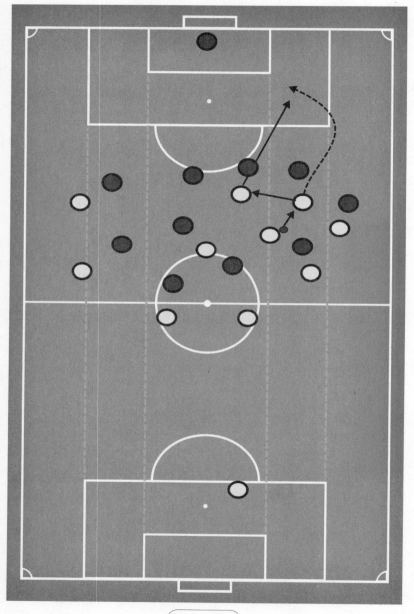

Figure 98

We have already seen with the chapters on the likes of Leroy Sane and Bernardo that the ability of the City wide forwards to play in quick combinations in tight areas creates opportunities to play behind the defensive line.

The importance of these players to be able to play in these areas, in combinations that are almost automatic, should not be overlooked. These movements and passes are a key aspect of the attacking side of the game model that has been put in place by Pep Guardiola.

Figure 98 will show another example of this kind of combination in action. As the right sided '8', Ilkay Gundogan has the ball and Raheem Sterling is only positioned just ahead of him. This is obviously not optimal given that there are other spaces in advanced areas that could have been taken up by the wide forward.

As Sterling takes possession, however, he shifts it quickly to Sergio Aguero who is playing as the forward. We then see Sterling spin outside the defender at speed moving in towards the edge of the penalty area. He is able to pick up the return pass from Aguero beyond the line of the defensive unit.

In terms of pure potential there are few players in this City squad who possess a higher ceiling than Raheem Sterling. Perhaps Phil Foden but he has a long way to go to reach the level of Sterling. Now, as a 24-year-old, the forward player is still some way from reaching his peak. It is extremely impressive that he has added layers to his game that many did not think he had. His improved understanding of where to find and how to attack space in the final third has seen him become one of the most impressive attacking players in football. It is clear for us all to see now just why Sterling is a key part of this squad of players and why Guardiola counts on him as much as he does.

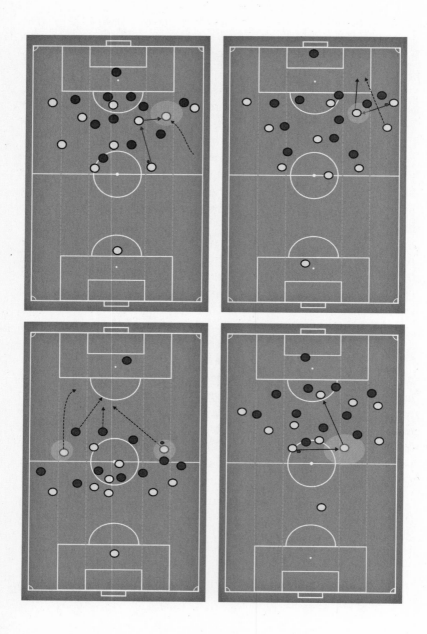

Chapter 16

Anatomy of a Goal

As we come to the end of this book we have now examined the tactical concepts that have been integral to the success enjoyed over the last two seasons by Pep Guardiola and Manchester City. We have also isolated and looked at the functions of some key individual players within these concepts. In order to tie everything together, we have decided to choose ten goals scored by City during this time period. Each goal displays the concepts that we have discussed over the course of the book and shows just how effective these concepts can be in breaking down opposition teams.

We should be clear, however, that these goals do not necessarily represent the ten best goals scored by City during this period. Nor are they presented in any form of ranked order. As with so many other things when it comes to Manchester City, sometimes these goals, and their general attacking play, should just be enjoyed and not ranked and rated.

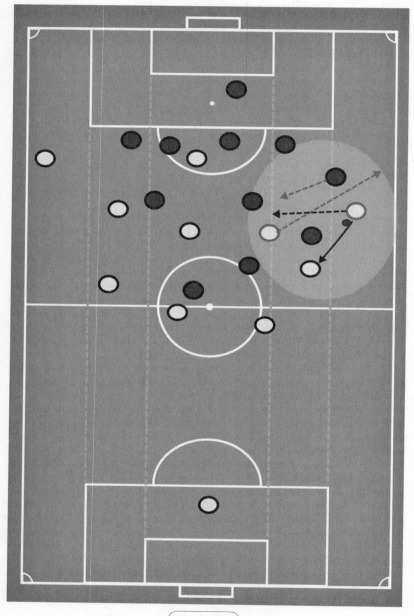

Figure 99

Goal One: Bernardo, Manchester City v Manchester United, 24.04.19

This goal came at a point in the season when Manchester United were struggling for form. In the lead-up to the match, there was a feeling that United may be able to take at least a point from their city rivals. Given the picture in the title race at this time, with Liverpool keeping pace with City, a draw in this match could have been fatal to City's title hopes.

Instead, United were relatively easily swept aside as City dominated the match and the ball to ensure that their rivals could not hurt them. This goal scored by Bernardo, while he was playing as the right-sided '8', showcased the intelligent movement and occupation of positions that we have seen in chapters looking closely at the Portuguese player but also Raheem Sterling.

In *figure 99*, we see the moment at which City break through to create the goalscoring opportunity. The ball is initially with Sterling, wide right, and he plays it back into Kyle Walker, who is narrow in the half-space. We then see Sterling make a decoy run inside to empty space in the wide area. This space is occupied by Bernardo making the run from inside to out to pick up possession of the ball before driving at the penalty area and shooting for goal.

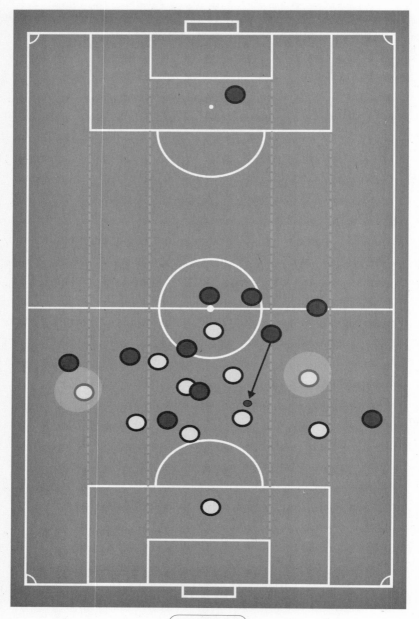

Figure 100

Goal Two: Leroy Sane, Manchester City v Manchester United, 24.04.19

To start this chapter with two goals from the same match, against City's biggest rivals, was not a deliberate act. It was, instead, a result of these two goals showcasing the way that City utilise their tactical concepts in order to break through the opposition.

Figure 100 shows us the moment at which City were able to win the ball back from United as they were trying to work it forwards towards the edge of the City penalty area. We see the defensive compactness from City as they have dropped into an established defensive shape in order to deny United the space in which they can play. We have also highlighted the positioning in this defensive block of the two wide players, Raheem Sterling on the right and Leroy Sane on the left. The United player makes a poor pass that is intercepted by Vincent Kompany and from there City can play quickly in transition.

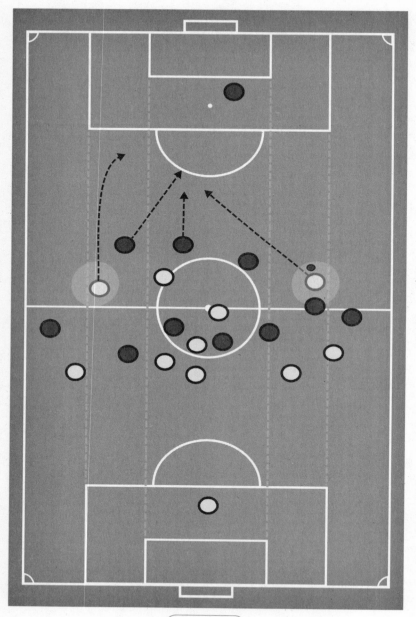

Figure 101

Now we see the play as it has developed in that transition. As soon as City won the ball back and began their attack we saw Leroy Sane on the left look to accelerate into space. The ball was immediately fed into Raheem Sterling who then turned and drove towards the opposition penalty area. As the entire structure of the game breaks down, with the opposition trying to stream back, we see Sterling calmly drive into the central areas. He chooses the right time to pause and allow the defensive players to collapse back beyond the ball and then plays the pass through to Sane for the German to finish.

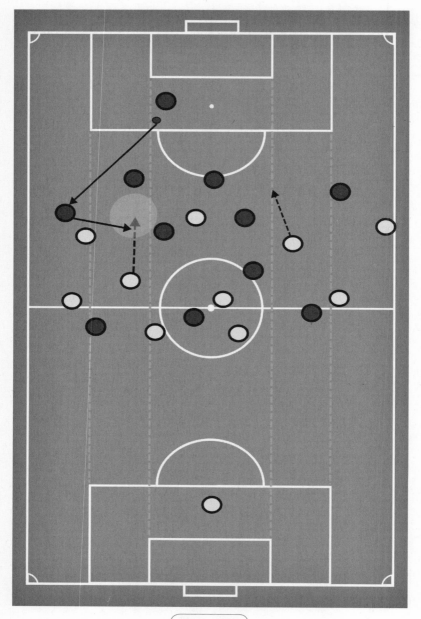

Figure 102

Goal Three: Bernardo, Manchester City v Fulham, 30.03.19

This goal was a direct result of the willingness of City players to press forward and engage the ball as their opposition were poorly positioned in their build-up phase. As the ball progresses initially from Sergio Rico in the Fulham goal he plays out to the right. City have adopted positions that are cutting off passing lanes that would allow Fulham to play forward. As such, the man receiving the ball looks to play back inside. However, the pass is loose and Kevin De Bruyne is on hand to anticipate this and win the ball quickly in a dangerous area.

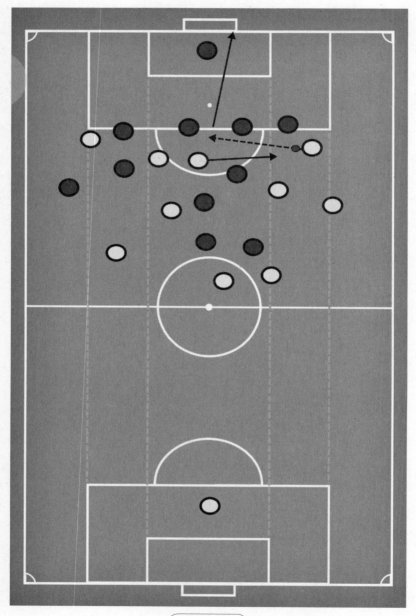

Figure 103

As the play then progresses from that area it is fed into Sergio Aguero in a central position outside of the penalty area. He does not have the space needed to shoot or access the penalty area and instead feeds the ball to Bernardo on the City right side. As we have already seen when discussing the Portuguese attacker in a previous chapter, he likes to drive inside at pace in possession of the ball. He does so here and when space opens, he drives the ball through for a goal.

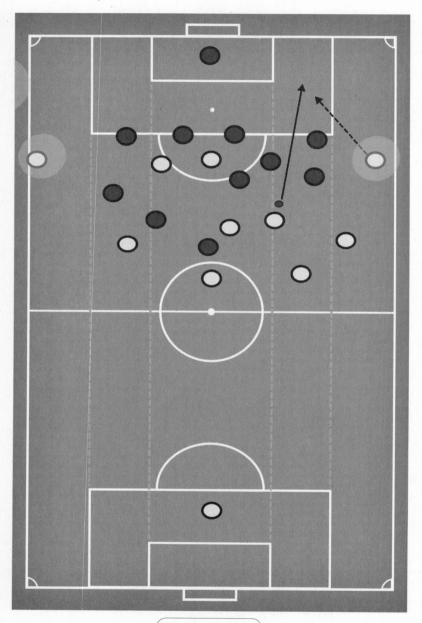

Figure one 104

Goal Four: Raheem Sterling, Manchester City v Chelsea, 10.02.19

This goal comes from a free kick to City in the right-sided half-space. With Kevin De Bruyne over the ball, we see Chelsea switch off as they look to adopt their defensive shape. Bernardo and Raheem Sterling are positioned extremely wide and high and these positions are not covered properly by the Chelsea defensive structure. In *figure 104* Bernardo makes an early angled run; De Bruyne sees this run and plays the ball through the space between defensive players into the penalty area. This simple run and pass is all that it took for City to create a goalscoring opportunity.

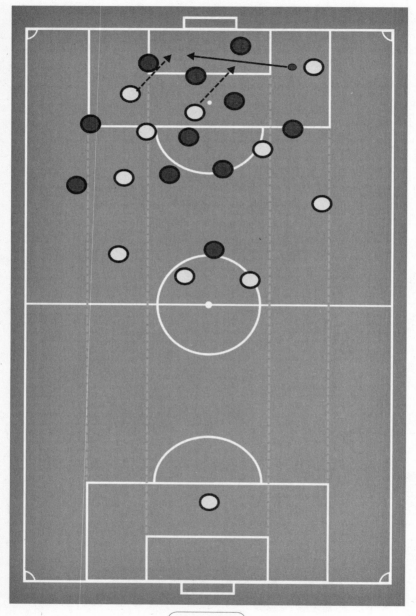

Figure 105

We can see in *figure 105* that as the play develops from this area we see Bernardo enter the corner of the penalty area into a very dangerous area. Sergio Aguero makes the run to the front post and Raheem Sterling has closed the space to attack the far post. The ball is easily played across the face of goal and Sterling is able to score.

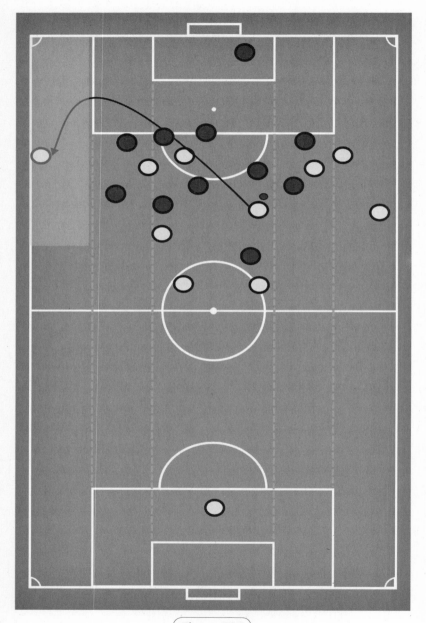

Figure 106

Goal Five: Sergio Aguero, Manchester City v Arsenal, 03.02.19

This goal was created while Arsenal were set in a compact block. We can see that City have created an overload on the right side of the field and Raheem Sterling is isolated out on the left-hand side. *Figure 106* shows this as the ball is switched over to the isolated side of the pitch where Sterling is able to pick up possession of the ball and drive into the corner of the penalty area. From this position, he combines quickly with a deeper team-mate and is able to get in behind the defensive block. From that position, the ball can simply be played across the face of goal for Sergio Aguero to tap it in.

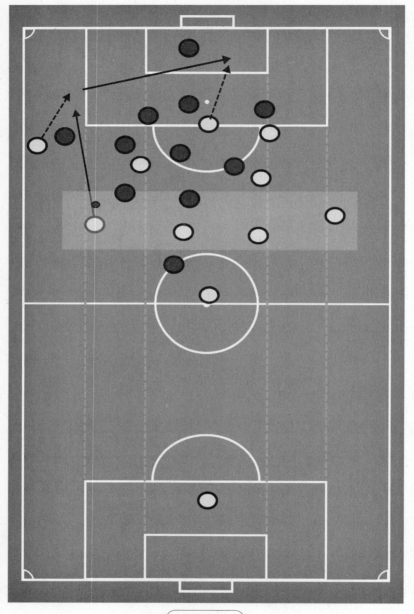

Figure 107

Goal Six: Gabriel Jesus, Manchester City v Wolves, 14.01.19

The key focal point of the attack for Manchester City is, of course, the striker at the tip of the three-man attack. While Sergio Aguero is the undisputed first-choice forward we also saw strong performances from Gabriel Jesus, with the Brazilian displaying similar movement and traits to Aguero.

In *figure 107* we, first of all, see the base from which City are able to build their attack. The two full-backs and one of the two central defenders are spread across the width of the pitch on the same line as the '6'. This line gives City the capacity to spread the ball across the field in order to identify the spaces and channels that can be used to play the ball forward. With the left-back in possession of the ball, he has the passing lane open to him in order to progress the ball forward.

As the ball is played between the opposition full-back and central defender, City create an extremely dangerous platform from which they can attack. As the ball moves into the penalty area we again see them play across the face of goal for Gabriel Jesus to easily finish in front of goal.

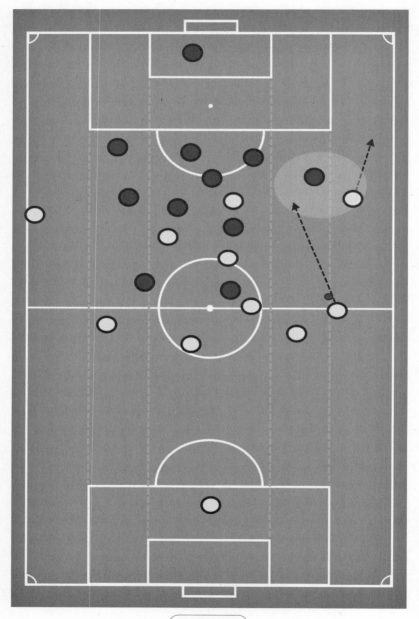

Figure 108

Goal Seven: David Silva, Manchester City v West Ham, 24.11.18

The key to this goal comes from the run that is made by Kyle Walker from right-back into the right-sided half-space. We see this run in *figure 108* as Walker, in possession, has a player wide to the right. Instead of simply playing the ball forward when he is not under pressure or trying to run outside where there is less space, we see Walker make an intelligent movement.

His run inside into the half-space isolates the single defensive player between the ball and the man in the wide area.

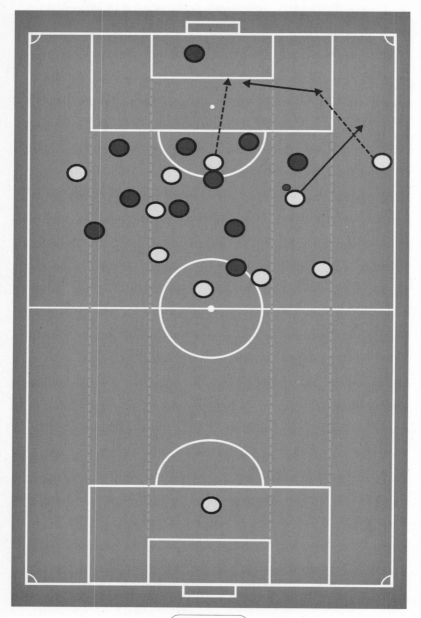

Figure 109

As the play develops we see the outcome in *figure 109*. The defensive player who had been isolated is forced to move inside to engage Kyle Walker and the ball. As the defender makes this choice we see Walker simply switch the ball outside for the right-sided forward to collect the ball and drive into the penalty area.

As this run is made, David Silva is the central player who continues his run and times it to move beyond the defensive player, meeting the ball as it is crossed into the central area.

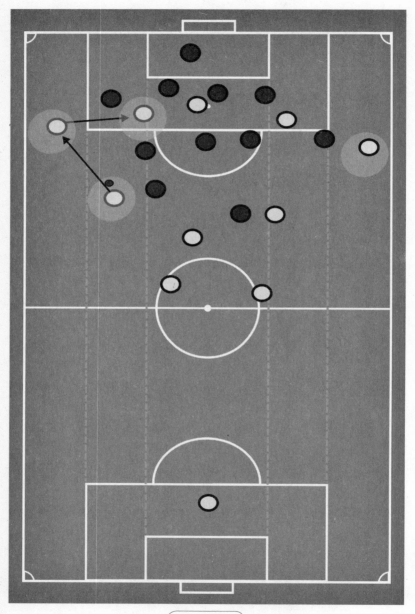

Figure 110

Goal Eight: Sergio Aguero, Manchester City v Burnley, 20.10.18

In *figure 110* we see the ball initially in the left half-space with Aymeric Laporte having advanced from left-back. We have also highlighted the positions of the two wide forwards and of David Silva who is playing ahead of Laporte in the same zone as the '8'. The ball is progressed first of all out to the left-wing where Raheem Sterling is able to collect possession. As the opposition then close in to engage the ball, Sterling quickly combines with a pass inside to Silva.

The positions that were taken up by the three City players, as shown above, are perfect to allow the ball to be progressed through and into the gaps in the opposition defensive structure.

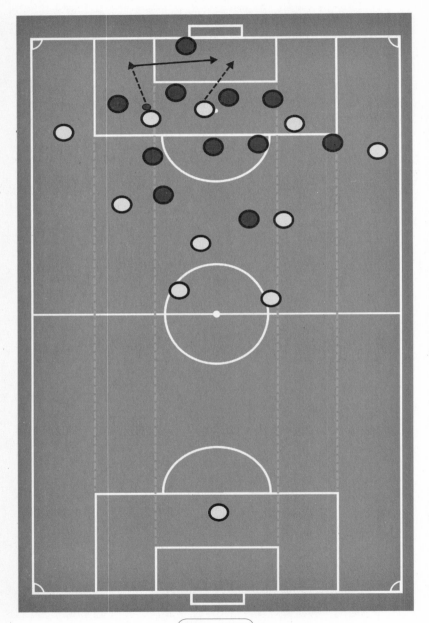

Figure 111

From that area, as we can see in *figure 111*, the play progresses quickly with the capacity of David Silva to manipulate the ball in these wide spaces in order to break through the last defender to the space wide of goal.

As we have already seen over and over in this chapter, that space allows Silva to pass the ball calmly across the face of goal for Sergio Aguero to steal in and finish.

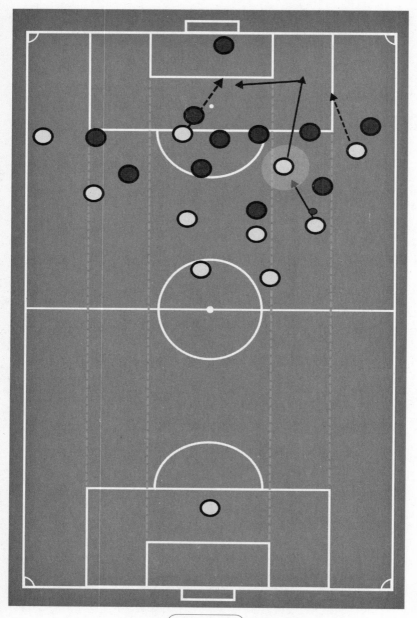

Figure 112

Goal Nine: Sergio Aguero, Manchester City v Cardiff City, 22.09.18

The ninth goal in our list once again showcases the importance of City occupying and playing in the half-spaces as they look to attack into the opposition penalty area. We can see in *figure 112* the ball is progressed from Kyle Walker, on a deeper line in the half-space, to Bernardo, on a higher line in the same lane. This pass is simple and allows City to progress the ball forward into an area where they can threaten the opposition defensive third.

The ball is then played quickly through the space between the two defensive players, with Raheem Sterling starting his diagonal run into the penalty area as soon as Bernardo has taken possession. As Sterling collects possession in the penalty area, Sergio Aguero has already made his run in the central spaces in order to get in front of the defenders. This allows the ball to be played across again for a simple finish.

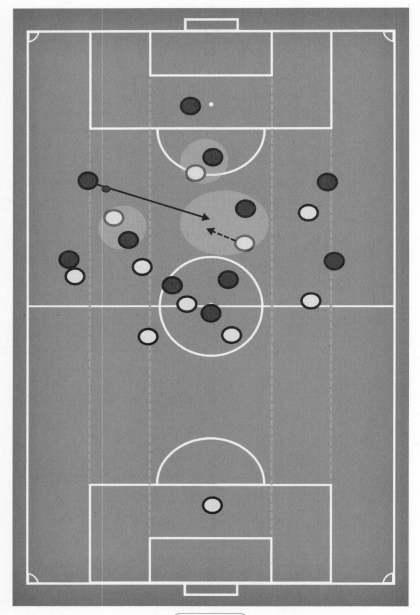

Figure 113

Goal Ten: Leroy Sane, Manchester City v Fulham, 15.09.18

The final goal in our list again comes from a situation in which the opposition had possession of the ball, and once again it is Fulham, although in a different match. We can see the situation in *figure 113* as Fulham are looking to build out from the back.

The key is in the fact that the two closest passing options for the man receiving the ball are taken away by City closely man marking them, as we saw in our chapter looking at cutting passing lanes. That results in the Fulham player trying to force a ball into central areas. This is a passing lane that had been deliberately left open by City and as the ball is played to this area we see Kevin De Bruyne move to close down the ball and force a turnover.

This then leads to Leroy Sane making a quick diagonal movement to allow the Belgian to play him through on goal for a comfortable finish.

So there we have it. Ten goals that encapsulate the concepts that we have discussed and examined over the course of this book. Once more we see that these concepts are not difficult and not complicated but they are executed extremely well and are difficult to defend against for the opposition.

Conclusion

In the years to come these Manchester City sides of 2017/18 and 2018/19 will go down as two of the best to ever play the game. The points tallies, the goals and the assists are part of the larger picture, but what underpins it all is the way that they play. The effortless manner with which they bypass defensive blocks or play quick combinations to isolate and then play past defenders is simply breathtaking.

We have to be clear, though: to some extent, luck also plays its part. City would not have retained their league title in the 2018/19 season were it not for a 1-0 home win against Leicester City in the penultimate match of the campaign. The source of this goal? A hugely improbable strike from distance from their captain and central defender Vincent Kompany when he strode out of defence in possession of the ball.

A goal of this type shows the other side of the game; you can implement tactical concepts as part of your game model but you also need to be flexible enough to alter your style as the moment demands. After this match, the likes of Raheem Sterling and Pep Guardiola were interviewed and asked what they were thinking as Kompany lined up the shot. Both had the same, or at least very similar, answers. 'No! Vinny, don't shoot!'

Within the game model that City use, a player in this area will look to progress the ball towards the penalty area to create a goalscoring opportunity with a higher chance of success than this shot. That Kompany not only attempted this shot but also succeeded, shows us that tactics remain only a part of the overall environment of football. This may seem strange after I have offered you an entire book discussing the tactical concepts of the game, but to truly appreciate the tactical side of football you have to be able to appreciate that other side as well.

A large part of what makes me love football is that it is so subjective. You and I could sit side by side and watch the same match but other than the objective truth, the score, we could come away with a vastly different take on what happened during the game. That doesn't necessarily mean that either of us would be wrong, simply that we have different views.

My hope is that this book has been interesting and useful to you in your understanding and enjoyment of the beautiful game. For those of you who already had an interest in the tactical side of football, then I hope this has built upon that interest and that you now want to try writing about and analysing the game for yourself. If I can do it then anyone can, right?

For those of you that felt that tactical writing contained too much 'jargon' and was overcomplicated then I hope that I have dispelled this myth and helped you to gain an interest in tactics.

For all of you that do not easily fall into either category then I simply hope that you enjoyed this book as much as I enjoyed writing it.